Introduction to Search with Sphinx

Introduction to Search with Sphinx

Andrew Aksyonoff

O'REILLY®

Beijing · Cambridge · Farnham · Köln · Sebastopol · Tokyo

Introduction to Search with Sphinx

by Andrew Aksyonoff

Published by O'Reilly Media, Inc., 1005 Gravenstein Highway North, Sebastopol, CA 95472.

O'Reilly books may be purchased for educational, business, or sales promotional use. Online editions are also available for most titles (*http://my.safaribooksonline.com*). For more information, contact our corporate/institutional sales department: (800) 998-9938 or *corporate@oreilly.com*.

Editor: Andy Oram		**Cover Designer:** Karen Montgomery	
Production Editor: Jasmine Perez		**Interior Designer:** David Futato	
Copyeditor: Audrey Doyle		**Illustrator:** Robert Romano	
Proofreader: Jasmine Perez			

Printing History:

April 2011:	First Edition.

ISBN: 978-0-596-80955-3

[LSI]

1302882733

Table of Contents

Preface

I can't quite believe it, but just 10 years ago there was no Google.

Other web search engines were around back then, such as AltaVista, HotBot, Inktomi, and AllTheWeb, among others. So the stunningly swift ascendance of Google can settle in my mind, given some effort. But what's even more unbelievable is that just 20 years ago there were no web search engines at all. That's only logical, because there was barely any Web! But it's still hardly believable today.

The world is rapidly changing. The volume of information available and the connection bandwidth that gives us access to that information grows substantially every year, making all the kinds—and volumes!—of data increasingly accessible. A 1-million-row database of geographical locations, which was mind-blowing 20 years ago, is now something a fourth-grader can quickly fetch off the Internet and play with on his netbook. But the processing rate at which human beings can consume information does not change much (and said fourth-grader would still likely have to read complex location names one syllable at a time). This inevitably transforms searching from something that only eggheads would ever care about to something that every single one of us has to deal with on a daily basis.

Where does this leave the application developers for whom this book is written? Searching changes from a high-end, optional feature to an essential functionality that absolutely has to be provided to end users. People trained by Google no longer expect a 50-component form with check boxes, radio buttons, drop-down lists, roll-outs, and every other bell and whistle that clutters an application GUI to the point where it resembles a Boeing 797 pilot deck. They now expect a simple, clean text search box.

But this simplicity is an illusion. A whole lot is happening under the hood of that text search box. There are a lot of different usage scenarios, too: web searching, vertical searching such as product search, local email searching, image searching, and other search types. And while a search system such as Sphinx relieves you from the implementation details of complex, low-level, full-text index and query processing, you will still need to handle certain high-level tasks.

How exactly will the documents be split into keywords? How will the queries that might need additional syntax (such as **cats AND dogs**) work? How do you implement matching that is more advanced than just exact keyword matching? How do you rank the results so that the text that is most likely to interest the reader will pop up near the top of a 200-result list, and how do you apply your business requirements to that ranking? How do you maintain the search system instance? Show nicely formatted snippets to the user? Set up a cluster when your database grows past the point where it can be handled on a single machine? Identify and fix bottlenecks if queries start working slowly? These are only a few of all the questions that come up during development, which only you and your team can answer because the choices are specific to your particular application.

This book covers most of the basic Sphinx usage questions that arise in practice. I am not aiming to talk about *all* the tricky bits and visit all the dark corners; because Sphinx is currently evolving so rapidly that even the online documentation lags behind the software, I don't think comprehensiveness is even possible. What I do aim to create is a practical field manual that teaches you how to use Sphinx from a basic to an advanced level.

Audience

I assume that readers have a basic familiarity with tools for system administrators and programmers, including the command line and simple SQL. Programming examples are in PHP, because of its popularity for website development.

Organization of This Book

This book consists of six chapters, organized as follows:

- Chapter 1, *The World of Text Search*, lays out the types of search and the concepts you need to understand regarding the particular ways Sphinx conducts searches.
- Chapter 2, *Getting Started with Sphinx*, tells you how to install and configure Sphinx, and run a few basic tests.
- Chapter 3, *Basic Indexing*, shows you how to set up Sphinx indexing for either an SQL database or XML data, and includes some special topics such as handling different character sets.
- Chapter 4, *Basic Searching*, describes the syntax of search text, which can be exposed to the end user or generated from an application, and the effects of various search options.
- Chapter 5, *Managing Indexes*, offers strategies for dealing with large data sets (which means nearly any real-life data set, such as multi-index searching).
- Chapter 6, *Relevance and Ranking*, gives you some guidelines for the crucial goal of presenting the best results to the user first.

Conventions Used in This Book

The following typographical conventions are used in this book:

Italic

> Indicates new terms, URLs, filenames, Unix utilities, and command-line options

`Constant width`

> Indicates variables and other code elements, the contents of files, and the output from commands

`Constant width bold`

> Shows commands or other text that should be typed literally by the user (such as the contents of full-text queries)

`Constant width italic`

> Shows text that should be replaced with user-supplied values

 This icon signifies a tip, suggestion, or general note.

Using Code Examples

This book is here to help you get your job done. In general, you may use the code in this book in your programs and documentation. You do not need to contact us for permission unless you're reproducing a significant portion of the code. For example, writing a program that uses several chunks of code from this book does not require permission. Selling or distributing a CD-ROM of examples from O'Reilly books *does* require permission. Answering a question by citing this book and quoting example code does not require permission. Incorporating a significant amount of example code from this book into your product's documentation *does* require permission.

We appreciate, but do not require, attribution. An attribution usually includes the title, author, publisher, and ISBN. For example: "*Introduction to Search with Sphinx*, by Andrew Aksyonoff. Copyright 2011 Andrew Aksyonoff, 978-0-596-80955-3."

If you feel your use of code examples falls outside fair use or the permission given here, feel free to contact us at *permissions@oreilly.com*.

We'd Like to Hear from You

Every example in this book has been tested on various platforms, but occasionally you may encounter problems. The information in this book has also been verified at each step of the production process. However, mistakes and oversights can occur and we will gratefully receive details of any you find, as well as any suggestions you would like to make for future editions. You can contact the authors and editors at:

O'Reilly Media, Inc.
1005 Gravenstein Highway North
Sebastopol, CA 95472
(800) 998-9938 (in the United States or Canada)
(707) 829-0515 (international or local)
(707) 829-0104 (fax)

We have a web page for this book, where we list errata, examples, and any additional information. You can access this page at:

http://www.oreilly.com/catalog/9780596809553

To comment or ask technical questions about this book, send email to the following address, mentioning the book's ISBN (978-0-596-80955-3 (http://www.oreilly.com/cat alog/%3CBOOK)):

bookquestions@oreilly.com

For more information about our books, courses, conferences, and news, see our website at http://www.oreilly.com.

Find us on Facebook: http://facebook.com/oreilly

Follow us on Twitter: http://twitter.com/oreillymedia

Watch us on YouTube: http://www.youtube.com/oreillymedia

Safari® Books Online

Safari Books Online is an on-demand digital library that lets you easily search over 7,500 technology and creative reference books and videos to find the answers you need quickly.

With a subscription, you can read any page and watch any video from our library online. Read books on your cell phone and mobile devices. Access new titles before they are available for print, and get exclusive access to manuscripts in development and post feedback for the authors. Copy and paste code samples, organize your favorites, download chapters, bookmark key sections, create notes, print out pages, and benefit from tons of other time-saving features.

O'Reilly Media has uploaded this book to the Safari Books Online service. To have full digital access to this book and others on similar topics from O'Reilly and other publishers, sign up for free at http://my.safaribooksonline.com.

Acknowledgments

Special thanks are due to Peter Zaitsev for all his help with the Sphinx project over the years and to Andy Oram for being both very committed and patient while making the book happen. I would also like to thank the rest of the O'Reilly team involved and, last but not least, the rest of the Sphinx team.

CHAPTER 1

The World of Text Search

Words frequently have different meanings, and this is evident even in the short description of Sphinx itself. We used to call it a *full-text search engine*, which is a standard term in the IT knowledge domain. Nevertheless, this occasionally delivered the wrong impression of Sphinx being either a Google-competing web service, or an embeddable software library that only hardened C++ programmers would ever manage to implement and use. So nowadays, we tend to call Sphinx a *search server* to stress that it's a suite of programs running on your hardware that you use to implement and maintain full-text searches, similar to how you use a database server to store and manipulate your data. Sphinx can serve you in a variety of different ways and help with quite a number of search-related tasks, and then some. The data sets range from indexing just a few blog posts to web-scale collections that contain billions of documents; workload levels vary from just a few searches per day on a deserted personal website to about 200 million queries per day on Craigslist; and query types fluctuate between simple quick queries that need to return top 10 matches on a given keyword and sophisticated analytical queries used for data mining tasks that combine thousands of keywords into a complex text query and add a few nontext conditions on top. So, there's a lot of things that Sphinx can do, and therefore a lot to discuss. But before we begin, let's ensure that we're on the same page in our dictionaries, and that the words I use mean the same to you, the reader.

Terms and Concepts in Search

Before exploring Sphinx in particular, let's begin with a quick overview of searching in general, and make sure we share an understanding of the common terms.

Searching in general can be formally defined as choosing a subset of entries that match given criteria from a complete data set. This is clearly too vague for any practical use, so let's look at the field to create a slightly more specific job description.

Thinking in Documents Versus Databases

Whatever unit of text you want to return is your *document*. A newspaper or journal may have articles, a government agency may have memoranda and notices, a content management system may have blogs and comments, and a forum may have threads and messages. Furthermore, depending on what people want in their search results, searchable documents can be defined differently. It might be desirable to find blog postings by comments, and so a document on a blog would include not just the post body but also the comments. On the other hand, matching an entire book by keywords is not of much use, and using a subsection or a page as a searchable unit of text makes much more sense. Each individual item that can come up in a search result is a document.

Instead of storing the actual text it indexes, Sphinx creates a full-text index that lets it efficiently search through that text. Sphinx can also store a limited amount of attached string data if you explicitly tell it to. Such data could contain the document's author, format, date of creation, and similar information. But, by default, the indexed text itself does not get stored. Under certain circumstances, it's possible to reconstruct the original text from the Sphinx index, but that's a complicated and computationally intensive task.

Thus, Sphinx stores a special data structure that represents the things we want to know about the document in a compressed form. For instance, because the word "programmer" appears over and over in this chapter, we wouldn't want to store each occurrence in the database. That not only would be a waste of space, but also would fail to record the information we're most interested in. Instead, our database would store the word "programmer" along with some useful statistics, such as the number of times it occurs in the document or the position it occupies each time.

Those journal articles, blog posts and comments, and other entities would normally be stored in a database. And, in fact, relational database terminology correlates well with a notion of the document in a full-text search system.

In a database, your data is stored in tables where you predefine a set of columns (ID, author, content, price, etc.) and then insert, update, or delete rows with data for those columns. Some of the data you store—such as author, price, or publication date—might not be part of the text itself; this metadata is called an *attribute* in Sphinx. Sphinx's full-text index is roughly equivalent to your data table, the full-text document is your row, and the document's searchable fields and attached attributes are your columns.

Database table ≈ Sphinx index

Database rows ≈ Sphinx documents

Database columns ≈ Sphinx fields and attributes

So, in these terms, how does a search query basically work—from a really high-level perspective?

When processing the user's request, Sphinx uses a *full-text index* to quickly look at each *full-text match*, that is, a document that matches all the specified keywords. It can then examine additional, nonkeyword-based searching conditions, if any, such as a restriction by blog post year, product price range, and so forth, to see whether it should be returned. The current document being examined is called a *candidate* document. Candidates that satisfy all the search criteria, whether keywords or not, are called *matches*. (Obviously, if there are no additional restrictions, all full-text matches just become matches.) Matches are then *ranked*, that is, Sphinx computes and attaches a certain relevance value, orders matches by that value, and returns the top *N* best matches to a calling application. Those top *N* most relevant matches (the top 1,000 by default) are collectively called a *result set*.

Why Do We Need Full-Text Indexes?

Why not just store the document data and then look for keywords in it when doing the searching? The answer is very simple: performance.

Looking for a keyword in document data is like reading an entire book cover to cover while watching out for keywords you are interested in. Books with concordances are much more convenient: with a concordance you can look up pages and sentences you need by keyword in no time.

The full-text index over a document collection is exactly such a concordance. Interestingly, that's not just a metaphor, but a pretty accurate or even literally correct description. The most efficient approach to maintaining full-text indexes, called *inverted files* and used in Sphinx as well as most other systems, works exactly like a book's index: for every given keyword, the inverted file maintains a sorted list of document identifiers, and uses that to match documents by keyword very quickly.

Query Languages

In order to meet modern users' expectations, search engines must offer more than searches for a string of words. They allow relationships to be specified through a query language whose syntax allows for special search operators.

For instance, virtually all search engines recognize the keywords AND and NOT as Boolean operators. Other examples of query language syntax will appear as we move through this chapter.

There is no standard query language, especially when it comes to more advanced features. Every search system uses its own syntax and defaults. For example, Google and Sphinx default to AND as an implicit operator, that is, they try to match all keywords by default; Lucene defaults to OR and matches any of the keywords submitted.

Logical Versus Full-Text Conditions

Search engines use two types of criteria for matching documents to the user's search.

Logical conditions

Logical conditions return a Boolean result based on an expression supplied by the user.

Logical expressions can get quite complex, potentially involving multiple columns, mathematical operations on columns, functions, and so on. Examples include:

```
price<100
LENGTH(title)>=20
(author_id=123 AND YEAROF(date_added)>=2000)
```

Both text, such as the `title` in the second example, and metadata, such as the `date_added` in the third example, can be manipulated by logical expressions. The third example illustrates the sophistication permitted by logical expressions. It includes the `AND` Boolean operator, the `YEAROF` function that presumably extracts the year from a date, and two mathematical comparisons.

Optional additional conditions of a full-text criterion can be imposed based on either the existence or the nonexistence of a keyword within a row (`cat AND dog BUT NOT mouse`), or on the positions of the matching keywords within a matching row (a phrase searching for "`John Doe`").

Because a logical expression evaluates to a Boolean true or false result, we can compute that result for every candidate row we're processing, and then either include or exclude it from the result set.

Full-text queries

The full-text type of search breaks down into a number of subtypes, applicable in different scenarios. These all fall under the general category of *keyword searching*.

Boolean search
> This is a kind of logical expression, but full-text queries use a narrower range of conditions that simply check whether a keyword occurs in the document. For example, `cat AND dog`, where `AND` is a Boolean operator, matches every document that mentions both "cat" and "dog," no matter where the keywords occur in the document. Similarly, `cat AND NOT dog`, where `NOT` is also an operator, will match every document that mentions "cat" but does not mention "dog" anywhere.

Phrase search
> This helps when you are looking for an exact match of a multiple-keyword quote such as "To be or not to be," instead of just trying to find each keyword by itself in no particular order. The de facto standard syntax for phrase searches, supported across all modern search systems, is to put quotes around the query (e.g., "`black cat`"). Note how, in this case, unlike in just Boolean searching, we need to know

not only that the keyword occurred in the document, but also where it occurred. Otherwise, we wouldn't know whether "black" and "cat" are adjacent. So, for phrase searching to work, we need our full-text index to store not just keyword-to-document mappings, but keyword *positions* within documents as well.

Proximity search

This is even more flexible than phrase searching, using positions to match documents where the keywords occur within a given distance to one another. Specific proximity query syntaxes differ across systems. For example, a proximity query in Sphinx would look like this:

```
"cat dog"~5
```

This means "find all documents where 'cat' and 'dog' occur within the same five keywords."

Field-based search

This is also known as field searching. Documents almost always have more than one field, and programmers frequently want to limit parts of a search to a given field. For example, you might want to find all email messages from someone named Peter that mention MySQL in the subject line. Syntaxes for this differ; the Sphinx phrase for this one would be:

```
@from Peter @subject MySQL
```

Most search systems let you combine these query types (or subquery types, as they are sometimes called) in the query language.

Differences between logical and full-text searches

One can think of these two types of searches as follows: logical criteria use entire columns as values, while full-text criteria implicitly split the text columns into arrays of words, and then work with those words and their position, matching them to a text query.

This isn't a mathematically correct definition. One could immediately argue that, as long as our "logical" criterion definition allows us to use functions, we can introduce a function `EXPLODE()` that takes the entire column as its argument and returns an array of word-position pairs. We could then express all full-text conditions in terms of set-theoretical operations over the results of `EXPLODE()`, therefore showing that all "full-text" criteria are in fact "logical." A completely unambiguous distinction in the mathematical sense would be 10 pages long, but because this book is not a Ph.D. dissertation, I will omit the 10-page definition of an `EXPLODE()` class of functions, and just keep my fingers crossed that the difference between logical and full-text conditions is clear enough here.

Natural Language Processing

Natural language processing (NLP) works very differently from keyword searches. NLP tries to capture the *meaning* of a user query, and answer the question instead of merely matching the keywords. For example, the query what POTUS number was JFK would ideally match a document saying "John Fitzgerald Kennedy, 35th U.S. president," even though it does not have any of the query keywords.

Natural language searching is a field with a long history that is still evolving rapidly. Ultimately, it is all about so-called *semantic analysis*, which means making the machine understand the general meaning of documents and queries, an algorithmically complex and computationally difficult problem. (The hardest part is the general semantic analysis of lengthy documents when indexing them, as search queries are typically rather short, making them a lot easier to process.)

NLP is a field of science worth a bookshelf in itself, and it is not the topic of this book. But a high-level overview may help to shine light on general trends in search. Despite the sheer general complexity of a problem, a number of different techniques to tackle it have already been developed.

Of course, general-purpose AI that can read a text and understand it is very hard, but a number of handy and simple tricks based on regular keyword searching and logical conditions can go a long way. For instance, we might detect "what is X" queries and rewrite them in "X is" form. We can also capture well-known synonyms, such as JFK, and replace them with jfk OR (john AND kennedy) internally. We can make even more assumptions when implementing a specific vertical search. For instance, the query 2br in reading on a property search website is pretty unambiguous: we can be fairly sure that "2br" means a two-bedroom apartment, and that the "in reading" part refers to a town named Reading rather than the act of reading a book, so we can adjust our query accordingly—say, replace "2br" with a logical condition on a number of bedrooms, and limit "reading" to location-related fields so that "reading room" in a description would not interfere.

Technically, this kind of query processing is already a form of query-level NLP, even though it is very simple.

From Text to Words

Search engines break down both documents and query text into particular keywords. This is called *tokenization*, and the part of the program doing it is called a *tokenizer* (or, sometimes, *word breaker*). Seemingly straightforward at first glance, tokenization has, in fact, so many nuances that, for example, Sphinx's tokenizer is one of its most complex parts.

The complexity arises out of a number of cases that must be handled. The tokenizer can't simply pay attention to English letters (or letters in any language), and consider everything else to be a separator. That would be too naïve for practical use. So the tokenizer also handles punctuation, special query syntax characters, special characters that need to be fully ignored, keyword length limits, and character translation tables for different languages, among other things.

We're saving the discussion of Sphinx's tokenizer features for later (a few of the most common features are covered in Chapter 3; a full discussion of all the advanced features is beyond the scope of this book), but one generic feature deserves to be mentioned here: *tokenizing exceptions*. These are individual words that you can anticipate must be treated in an unusual way. Examples are "C++" and "C#," which would normally be ignored because individual letters aren't recognized as search terms by most search engines, while punctuation such as plus signs and number signs are ignored. You want people to be able to search on C++ and C#, so you flag them as exceptions. A search system might or might not let you specify exceptions. This is no small issue for a jobs website whose search engine needs to distinguish C++ vacancies from C# vacancies and from pure C ones, or a local business search engine that does not want to match an "AT&T" query to the document "T-Mobile office AT corner of Jackson Rd. and Johnson Dr."

Linguistics Crash Course

Sphinx currently supports most common linguistics requirements, such as stemming (finding the root in words) and keyword substitution dictionaries. In this section, we'll explain what a language processor such as Sphinx can do for you so that you understand how to configure it and make the best use of its existing features as well as extend them if needed.

One important step toward better language support is *morphology processing*. We frequently want to match not only the exact keyword form, but also other forms that are related to our keyword—not just "cat" but also "cats"; not just "mouse" but also "mice"; not just "going" but also "go," "goes," "went," and so on. The set of all the word forms that share the same meaning is called the *lexeme*; the canonical word form that the search engine uses to represent the lexeme is called the *lemma*. In the three examples just listed, the lemmas would be "cat," "mouse," and "go," respectively. All the other variants of the root are said to "ascend" to this root. The process of converting a word to its lemma is called *lemmatization* (no wonder).

Lemmatization is not a trivial problem in itself, because natural languages do not strictly follow fixed rules, meaning they are rife with exceptions ("mice were caught"), tend to evolve over time ("i am blogging this"), and last but not least, are ambiguous, sometimes requiring the engine to analyze not only the word itself, but also a surrounding context ("the dove flew away" versus "she dove into the pool"). So an ideal lemmatizer would need to combine part-of-speech tagging, a number of algorithmic transformation rules, and a dictionary of exceptions.

That's pretty complex, so frequently, people use something simpler—namely, so-called *stemmers*. Unlike a lemmatizer, a stemmer intentionally does not aim to normalize a word into an exactly correct lemma. Instead, it aims to output a so-called *stem*, which is not even necessarily a correct word, but is chosen to be the same for all the words—and only those words—that ascend to a given morphological root. Stemmers, for the sake of performance, typically apply only a small number of processing rules; have only a few, if any, prerecorded exceptions; and ultimately do not aim to achieve 100 percent correct normalization.

The most popular stemmer for the English language is the Porter stemmer, developed by Martin Porter in 1979. Although pretty efficient and easy to implement, it suffers from normalization errors. One notorious example is the stemmer's reduction of "business" and "busy" to the same stem "busi," even though they have very different meanings and we'd rather keep them separate. This is, by the way, an example of how exceptions in natural language win the fight against rules: many other words are formed from a verb using a "-ness" suffix ("awareness", "forgiveness", etc.) and properly reduce to an original verb, but "business" is an exception. A smart lemmatizer would be able to keep "business" as a form on its own.

An even smarter lemmatizer would know that "the dove flew away" talks about a pigeon, and not diving. And this seemingly simple sample brings in a number of other linguistic concepts.

First, "dove" is a *synonym* for "pigeon." The words are different, but the meaning is similar or even almost identical, and that's exactly what synonyms are. Ornithologists can quibble, but in popular usage, these words are used interchangeably for many of the same kinds of birds. Synonyms can be less exact, such as "sick" and "ill" and "acquisitions" and "purchases," or they can be as complex an example as "put up the white flag" and "surrender."

Second, "dove" the noun is also a *homonym* for the simple past form of "dive" the verb. Homonyms are words that are spelled the same but have different meanings.

Third, in this example, we can't really detect whether it's "dove" the noun or "dove" the verb by the word itself. To do that, we need to perform *part-of-speech (POS) tagging*. That is, we need to analyze the entire sentence and find out whether the "dove" was a subject, a predicate, or something else—all of that to normalize our "dove" to a proper form.

Homonyms can, in fact, be an even bigger problem. POS tagging will not help to distinguish a "river bank" from a "savings bank" because both banks here are nouns. The process of telling one bank from the other is called *word-sense disambiguation* (WSD) and is (you bet) another open problem in computational linguistics.

Text processing of this depth is, of course, rather expensive in terms of both development costs and performance. So most of the currently available systems are limited to simpler functionality such as stemming or lemmatization, and do not do complex linguistic processing such as POS tagging or WSD. Major web search engines are one notable exception, as they strive for extreme quality—which brings us to the subject of relevance ranking.

Relevance, As Seen from Outer Space

Assume that we just found 1 million documents that match our query. We can't even glance at all of them, so we need to further narrow down our search somehow. We might want the documents that match the query "better" to be displayed first. But how does the search engine know that document A is better than document B with regard to query Q?

It does so with the aid of *relevance ranking*, which computes a certain relevance value, or *weight*, for every given document and given query. This weight can then be used to order matching documents.

Ranking is an open problem, and actually a rather tough one. Basically, different people can and do judge different documents as relevant or irrelevant to the same query. That means there can't be a single ideal suit-all relevance function that will always put an "ideal" result in the first position. It also means that generally better ranking can ultimately be achieved only by looking at lots of human-submitted grades, and trying to learn from them.

On the high end, the amount of data to process can be vast, with every document having hundreds or even thousands of ranking factors, some of which vary with every query, multiplied by millions of prerecorded human *assessors' judgments*, yielding billions of values to crunch on every given iteration of a gradient descent quest for a Holy Grail of 0.01 percent better relevance. So, manually examining the grade data cannot possibly work and an improved relevance function can realistically be computed only with the aid of state-of-the-art machine learning algorithms. Then the resultant function itself has to be analyzed using so-called *quality metrics*, because playing "hot or not" through a million grades assigned to each document and query isn't exactly realistic either. The bottom line is that if you want to join the Bing search quality group, learn some math, preferably lots of it, and get used to running lots of human factors labs.

On lower levels of search, not everyone needs all that complexity and a simple grokable relevance function could suffice. You still want to know how it works in Sphinx, what can be tweaked, and how to evaluate your tweaking results.

There's a lot to relevance in general, so I'll dedicate a separate chapter to discussing all things ranking, and all the nitty-gritty details about Sphinx ranking. For the purposes of providing an overview here, let me limit myself to mentioning that Sphinx supports several ranking functions, lets you choose among them on the fly, lets you tweak the outcome, and is friendly to people trying to hack new such functions into it. Oh yes, in some of the rankers it plays a few tricks to ensure quality, as per-quality metrics are closer to the high end than most search engines.

Result Set Postprocessing

Exaggerating a bit, relevance ranking is the only thing that general web search engine developers care about, because their end users only want a few pages that answer their query best, and that's it. Nobody sorts web pages by dates, right?

But for applications that most of us work on, embedded in more complex end-user tasks, additional result set processing is also frequently involved. You don't want to display a random iPhone to your product search engine user; he looks for the cheapest one in his area. You don't display a highly relevant article archived from before you were born as your number one news search result, at least not on the front page; the end user is likely searching for slightly fresher data. When there are 10,000 matches from a given site, you might want to cluster them. Searches might need to be restricted to a particular subforum, or an author, or a site. And so on.

All this calls for result set postprocessing. We find the matches and rank them, like a web search engine, but we also need to filter, sort, and group them. Or in SQL syntax, we frequently need additional WHERE, ORDER BY, and GROUP BY clauses on top of our search results.

Search engines frequently grow from web pages' tasks of indexing and searching, and might not support postprocessing at all, might support only an insufficient subset, might perform poorly, or might consume too many resources. Such search engines focus on, and mostly optimize for, relevance-based ordering. But in practice, it's definitely not enough to benchmark whether the engine quickly returns the first 10 matches sorted by relevance. Scanning 10,000 matches and ordering them by, say, price can result in a jaw-dropping difference in performance figures.

Sphinx, on the other hand, was designed to index content stored in a database from day one, and now it supports arithmetic expressions, WHERE, ORDER BY, and GROUP BY in full, very efficiently. In fact, Sphinx supports those functions literally: you can use good old SQL syntax to express your queries (refer to Chapter 4 for a detailed discussion). Moreover, Sphinx-side processing is so efficient that it can outperform a database on certain general (not just full-text!) SQL query types.

Full-Text Indexes

A search engine must maintain a special data structure in order to process search queries quickly. This type of structure is called a *full-text index*. Unsurprisingly, there's more than one way to implement this.

In terms of storage, the index can be stored on disk or exist only in RAM. When on disk, it is typically stored in a custom file format, but sometimes engines choose to use a database as a storage backend. The latter usually performs worse because of the additional database overhead.

The most popular conceptual data structure is a so-called *inverted file*, which consists of a dictionary of all keywords, a list of document IDs, and a list of the positions in the documents for every keyword. All this data is kept in sorted and compressed form, allowing for efficient queries.

The reason for keeping the position is to find out, for instance, that "John" and "Kennedy" occur side by side or very close to each other, and therefore are likely to satisfy a search for that name. Inverted files that keep keyword positions are called *word-level indexes*, while those that omit the positions are *document-level indexes*. Both kinds can store additional data along with document IDs—for instance, storing the number of keyword occurrences lets us compute statistical text rankings such as BM25. However, to implement phrase queries, proximity queries, and more advanced ranking, a word-level index is required.

Lists of keyword positions can also be called *occurrence lists*, *postings lists*, or *hit lists*. We will mostly use "document lists" and "hit lists" in the following description.

Another index structure, nowadays more of a historical than a practical interest, is a *signature file*, which keeps a bit vector of matching documents for every keyword. Signature files are very quick at answering Boolean queries with frequent keywords. However, for all the other types of queries, inverted files perform better. Also, signature files cannot contain keyword positions, meaning they don't support phrase queries and they have very limited support for text-based ranking (even the simple and classic BM25 is barely possible). That's a major constraint.

Depending on the compression scheme used, document-level indexes can be as compact as 7 to 10 percent of the original text size, and word-level indexes 30 to 40 percent of the text size. But in a full-text index, smaller is not necessarily better. First, more complex compression schemes take more CPU time to decompress, and might result in overall slower querying despite the savings in I/O traffic. Second, a bigger index might contain redundant information that helps specific query types. For instance, Sphinx keeps a redundant field mask in its document lists that consumes extra disk space and I/O time, but lets a fielded query quickly reject documents that match the keyword in the wrong field. So the Sphinx index format is not as compact as possible, consuming up to 60 to 70 percent of the text size at the time of this writing, but that's a conscious trade-off to get better querying speed.

Indexes also might carry additional per-keyword payloads such as *morphological information* (e.g., a payload attached to a root form can be an identifier of a particular specific word form that was reduced to this root), or *keyword context* such as font size, width, or color. Such payloads are normally used to improve relevance ranking.

Last but not least, an index format might allow for either *incremental updates* of the indexed data, or nonincremental index rebuilds only. An incremental index format can take partial data updates after it's built; a nonincremental one is essentially read-only after it's built. That's yet another trade-off, because structures allowing incremental updates are harder to implement and maintain, and therefore experience lower performance during both indexing and searching.

Sphinx currently supports two indexing backends that combine several of the features we have just discussed:

- Our most frequently used "regular" disk index format defaults to an on-disk, nonincremental, word-level inverted file. To avoid tedious rebuilds, you can combine multiple indexes in a single search, and do frequent rebuilds only on a small index with recently changed rows. Setting that up is discussed in detail in Chapter 5.
- That disk index format also lets you omit hit lists for either some or all keywords, leading to either a partial word-level index or a document-level index, respectively. This is essentially a performance versus quality trade-off.
- The other Sphinx indexing backend, called the RT (for "real time") index, is a hybrid solution that builds upon regular disk indexes, but also adds support for in-memory, incremental, word-level inverted files. So we try to combine the best of both worlds, that is, the instant incremental update speed of in-RAM indexes and the large-scale searching efficiency of on-disk nonincremental indexes.

Search Workflows

We've just done a 30,000-foot overview of different search-related areas. A modern scientific discipline called *Information Retrieval* (IR) studies all the areas we mentioned, and more. So, if you're interested in learning about the theory and technology of the modern search engines, including Sphinx, all the way down to the slightest details, IR books and papers are what you should refer to.

In this book we're focusing more on practice than on theory, that is, how to use Sphinx in scenarios of every kind. So, let's briefly review those scenarios.

Kinds of Data

Sphinx is a search engine and not a full-blown database just yet, so the raw data to be indexed is generally stored elsewhere. Usually you'd have an existing SQL database, or a collection of XML documents that you need indexed. When SQL and XML aren't efficient enough, the data might be stored in a custom data warehouse. In all these cases, we're talking about *structured data* that has preidentified text fields and nontext attributes. The columns in an SQL database and the elements in an XML document both impose some structure. The Sphinx document model is also structured, making it very easy to index and search such data. For instance, if your documents are in SQL, you just tell Sphinx what rows to fetch and what columns to index.

In the case of *unstructured data*, you will have to impose some structure yourself. When given a bunch of DOC, PDF, MP3, and AVI files, Sphinx is not able to automatically identify types, extract text based on type, and index that text. Instead, Sphinx needs you to pass the text and assign the field and attribute names. So you can still use it with unstructured data, but extracting the structure is up to you.

One extra requirement that Sphinx puts on data is that the units of data must have a *unique integer document identifier*, a.k.a. *docID*. The docID has to be a unique integer, not a string. Rows in the database frequently come with the necessary identifier when their primary key (PK) is an integer. It's not a big deal when they don't; you can generate some docIDs for Sphinx on the fly and store your string PK from the database (or XML document name) as an attribute.

Indexing Approaches

Different indexing approaches are best for different workflows. In a great many scenarios, it's sufficient to perform *batch indexing*, that is, to occasionally index a chunk of data. The batches being indexed might contain either the complete data, which is called *full reindexing*, or just the recently changed data, which is *delta reindexing*.

Although batching sounds slow, it really isn't. Reindexing a delta batch with a cron job every minute, for instance, means that new rows will become searchable in 30 seconds on average, and no more than 60 seconds. That's usually fine, even for such a dynamic application as an auction website.

When even a few seconds of delay is not an option, and data must become searchable instantly, you need *online indexing*, a.k.a. *real-time indexing*. Sometimes this is referred to as *incremental indexing*—though that isn't entirely formally correct.

Sphinx supports both approaches. Batch indexing is generally more efficient, but real-time indexing comes with a smaller indexing delay, and can be easier to maintain.

When there's just too much data for a single CPU core to handle, indexes will need to be *sharded* or *partitioned* into several smaller indexes. When there's way too much data for a single machine to handle, some of the data will have to be moved to other machines, and an index will have to become *distributed* across machines. This isn't fully automatic with Sphinx, but it's pretty easy to set up.

Finally, batch indexing does not necessarily need to be done on the same machine as the searches. It can be moved to a separate *indexing server*—either to avoid impacting searches while indexing takes place, or to avoid redundant indexing when several *index replicas* are needed for failover.

Full-Text Indexes and Attributes

Sphinx appends a few items to the regular RDBMS vocabulary, and it's essential to understand them. A relational database basically has tables, which consist of rows, which in turn consist of columns, where every column has a certain type, and that's pretty much it. Sphinx's full-text index also has rows, but they are called *documents*, and—unlike in the database—they are *required* to have a unique integer primary key (a.k.a. ID).

As we've seen, documents often come with a lot of metadata such as author information, publication data, or reviewer ranking. I've also explained that using this metadata to retrieve and order documents usefully is one of the great advantages of using a specialized search engine such as Sphinx. The metadata, or "attributes," as we've seen, are stored simply as extra fields next to the fields representing text.

Sphinx doesn't store the exact text of a document, but indexes it and stores the necessary data to match queries against it. In contrast, attributes are handled fairly simply: they are stored in their index fields verbatim, and can later be used for additional result set manipulation, such as sorting or grouping.

Thus, if you are indexing a table of book abstracts, you probably want to declare the book title and the abstract as full-text fields (to search through them using keywords), while declaring the book price, the year it was published, and similar metadata as attributes (to sort keyword search results by price or filter them by year).

Approaches to Searching

The way searches are performed is closely tied to the indexing architecture, and vice versa. In the simplest case, you would "just search"—that is, run a single *search query* on a single locally available index. When there are multiple indexes to be searched, the search engine needs to handle a *multi-index query*. Performing multiple search queries in one batch is a *multi-query*.

Search queries that utilize multiple cores on a single machine are *parallelized*—not to be confused with plain queries running in parallel with each other. Queries that need to reach out to other machines over the network are *distributed*.

Sphinx can do two major functional groups of search queries. First and foremost are *full-text queries* that match documents to keywords. Second are *full scans*, or *scan queries*, which loop through the attributes of all indexed documents and match them by attributes instead of keywords. An example of a scan is searching by just date range or author identifier and no keywords. When there are keywords to search for, Sphinx uses a full-text query.

One can emulate scans by attaching a special keyword to every row and searching for that row. Scans were introduced by user request when it turned out that, in some cases, even that emulated approach was more efficient than an equivalent SQL query against a database server.

Full-text queries can, in turn, either be just simple *bags of words*, or utilize the *query syntax* that Sphinx provides.

Kinds of Results

Queries that Sphinx sees are not necessarily exactly what the end user types in the search box. And correspondingly, both the search box and the results the end user sees might not be exactly what come out of Sphinx. You might choose to preprocess the raw queries coming from end users somehow.

For instance, when a search for all the words does not match, the application might analyze the query, pick keywords that did not match any documents, and rerun a *rewritten query* built without them. An application could also automatically perform *corrections* to keywords in which a typo is suspected.

Sometimes magic happens even before the query is received. This is often displayed as *query suggestions* in a search box as you type.

Search results aren't a list of numeric IDs either. When documents are less than ideally described by their title, abstract, or what have you, it's useful to display *snippets* (a.k.a. *excerpts*) in the search results. Showing additional navigational information (document types, price brackets, vendors, etc.), known as *facets*, can also come in handy.

CHAPTER 2

Getting Started with Sphinx

In this chapter, we will cover basic installation, configuration, and maintenance of Sphinx. Don't be fooled by the adjective "basic" and skip the chapter. By "basic," I don't mean something simple to the point of being obvious—instead, I mean features that literally everyone uses.

Sphinx, by default, uses MySQL as its source for data and assumes that you have both MySQL and the MySQL development libraries installed. You can certainly run Sphinx with some other relational database or data source, but MySQL is very popular and this chapter is based on it for convenience. There are at least half a dozen easy ways to install MySQL on most systems, so this chapter won't cover that task. I'll also assume you know some basic SQL.

Workflow Overview

Installation, configuration, and usage are all pieces of a larger picture. A complete search solution consists of four key components:

Your client program
> This accepts the user's search string (or builds a search string through its own criteria), sends a query to *searchd*, and displays the results.

A data source
> This stores your data and is queried by the *indexer* program. Most Sphinx sites use MySQL or another SQL server for storage. But that's not a fundamental requirement—Sphinx can work just as well with non-SQL data sources. And we'll see, in the following section, that you can populate Sphinx's index from an application instead of a fixed source such as a database.

indexer
> This program fetches the data from the data source and creates a full-text index of that data. You will need to run *indexer* periodically, depending on your specific requirements. For instance, an index over daily newspaper articles can naturally be built on a daily basis, just after every new issue is finished. An index over more

dynamic data can and should be rebuilt more frequently. For instance, you'd likely want to index auction items every minute.

searchd

This program talks to your (client) program, and uses the full-text index built by *indexer* to quickly process search queries. However, there's more to *searchd* than just searching. It also does result set processing (filtering, ordering, and grouping); it can talk to remote *searchd* copies and thus implement distributed searching; and besides searching, it provides a few other useful functions such as building snippets, splitting a given text into keywords (a.k.a. tokenizing), and other tasks.

So, the data more or less travels from the storage (the data source) to *indexer*, which builds the index and passes it to *searchd*, and then to your program. The first travel segment happens every time you run *indexer*, the second segment when indexing completes and *indexer* notifies *searchd*, and the final segment (i.e., to the program) every time you query. See Figure 2-1.

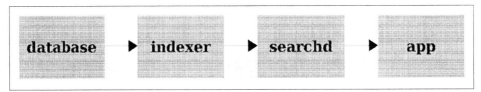

Figure 2-1. Data flow with Sphinx

We can also take a service-centric view instead of a data-centric view. In Figure 2-2, *searchd* is the continuously running server that you talk with, answering search queries in real time just as a relational database answers data queries. *indexer* is a separate tool that pulls the data, builds indexes, and passes them to *searchd*.

In essence, this is a "pull" model: *indexer* goes to the database, pulls the data, creates the index(es), and hands them to *searchd*. One important consequence of this is that Sphinx is storage engine, database, and generally data source agnostic. You can store your data using any built-in or external MySQL storage engine (MyISAM, InnoDB, ARCHIVE, PBXT, etc.), or in PostgreSQL, Oracle, MS SQL, Firebird, or not even in a database. As long as *indexer* can either directly query your database or receive XML content from a proxy program and get the data, it can index it.

Figure 2-1 and Figure 2-2 cover disk-based indexing on the backend only. With real-time indexes, the workflow is substantially different—*indexer* is never used, and data to index needs to be sent directly to *searchd* by either the application or the database.

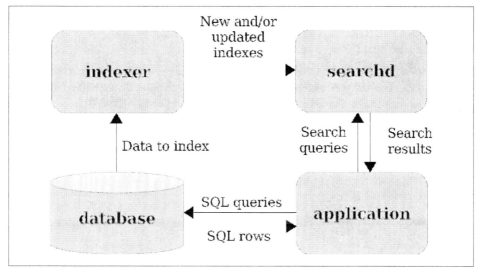

Figure 2-2. Database, Sphinx, and application interactions

Getting Started ... in a Minute

The easiest way to get Sphinx up and running is to install a binary package. That gets you a working deployment in almost literally one click. For good measure, it leaves you with a cheat sheet for how to run Sphinx.

```
[root@localhost ~]# rpm -i sphinx-1.10-1.el5.i386.rpm

Sphinx installed!
Now create a full-text index, start the search daemon, and you're all set.

To manage indexes:
    editor /etc/sphinx/sphinx.conf

To rebuild all disk indexes:
    sudo -u sphinx indexer --all --rotate

To start/stop search daemon:
    service searchd start/stop

To query search daemon using MySQL client:
    mysql -h 0 -P 9306
    mysql> SELECT * FROM test1 WHERE MATCH('test');

See the manual at /usr/share/doc/sphinx-1.10 for details.

For commercial support please contact Sphinx Technologies Inc at
http://sphinxsearch.com/contacts.html
```

A fresh RPM installation will install */etc/sphinx/sphinx.conf* and a sample configuration file preloaded with two test full-text indexes: a disk-based index called `test1`, and an RT index called `testrt`.

On Windows, or when installing manually from source, you can create *sphinx.conf* by copying one of the sample configuration file templates (those with a *.conf.in* extension) to it, and make these minimal edits so that the following tests will work:

- Replace `@CONFDIR@` with the pathnames where you plan to store your data and logs.
- Fill in the basic `sql_` parameters in the `src1` definition with the parameters you use to attach to MySQL. For the purposes of this chapter, I assume you're running on the same system and logging in to MySQL as the root user without a password. The parameters are therefore:

```
sql_host    = localhost
sql_user    = root
sql_pass    =
sql_db      = test
```

Sphinx binaries will normally look for *sphinx.conf* in a default location on your system, and then in a current directory. You can also override the *sphinx.conf* location during the binary's run using the `--config` command-line switch.

The `test1` index fetches its data from a sample MySQL table (`test.documents`), so in order to use it, you need to populate that table first, then run *indexer* to build the index data. Depending on your version of MySQL, you might have to create a *test* database manually. You can also use a different database name and substitute it for *test* in the following examples. You can load the table by loading the sample SQL dump *example.sql*, which was installed in */usr/share/doc*.

```
[root@localhost ~]# mysql -u root test < /usr/share/doc/sphinx-1.10/example.sql
[root@localhost ~]# indexer test1
Sphinx 1.10-id64-beta (r2420)
Copyright (c) 2001-2010, Andrew Aksyonoff
Copyright (c) 2008-2010, Sphinx Technologies Inc (http://sphinxsearch.com)

using config file '/etc/sphinx/sphinx.conf'...
indexing index 'test1'...
collected 4 docs, 0.0 MB
sorted 0.0 Mhits, 100.0% done
total 4 docs, 193 bytes
total 0.007 sec, 24683 bytes/sec, 511.57 docs/sec
total 3 reads, 0.000 sec, 0.1 kb/call avg, 0.0 msec/call avg
total 9 writes, 0.000 sec, 0.1 kb/call avg, 0.0 msec/call avg
```

You can then start *searchd* and query the indexes using either a sample PHP test program, or just a regular MySQL client:

```
[root@localhost ~]# service searchd start
Starting searchd: Sphinx 1.10-id64-beta (r2420)
Copyright (c) 2001-2010, Andrew Aksyonoff
Copyright (c) 2008-2010, Sphinx Technologies Inc (http://sphinxsearch.com)
```

```
using config file '/etc/sphinx/sphinx.conf'...
listening on all interfaces, port=9312
listening on all interfaces, port=9306
precaching index 'test1'
[root@localhost ~]# mysql -u root test < /usr/share/doc/sphinx-1.10/example.sql
precached 2 indexes in 0.005 sec
                                                          [  OK  ]
[root@localhost ~]# mysql -h0 -P9306
Welcome to the MySQL monitor.  Commands end with ; or \g.
Your MySQL connection id is 1
Server version: 1.10-id64-beta (r2420)

Type 'help;' or '\h' for help. Type '\c' to clear the buffer.

mysql> select * from test1 where match('test');
+------+--------+----------+------------+
| id   | weight | group_id | date_added |
+------+--------+----------+------------+
|    1 |   2421 |        1 | 1283729225 |
|    2 |   2421 |        1 | 1283729225 |
|    4 |   1442 |        2 | 1283729225 |
+------+--------+----------+------------+
3 rows in set (0.00 sec)

mysql> exit
Bye
[root@localhost ~]# php /usr/share/sphinx/api/test.php test
Query 'test ' retrieved 3 of 3 matches in 0.000 sec.
Query stats:
    'test' found 5 times in 3 documents

Matches:
1. doc_id=1, weight=101, group_id=1, date_added=2010-09-06 03:27:05
2. doc_id=2, weight=101, group_id=1, date_added=2010-09-06 03:27:05
3. doc_id=4, weight=1, group_id=2, date_added=2010-09-06 03:27:05
[root@localhost ~]#
```

RT indexes are even simpler. They get populated on the fly, so you don't need to have a database or run *indexer*. Just launch *searchd* and start working:

```
[root@localhost ~]# mysql -h0 -P9306
Welcome to the MySQL monitor.  Commands end with ; or \g.
Your MySQL connection id is 1
Server version: 1.10-id64-beta (r2420)

Type 'help;' or '\h' for help. Type '\c' to clear the buffer.

mysql> select * from testrt;
Empty set (0.00 sec)
```

Let's hold it right there for a second, and fix your attention on something elusive but very important.

This is not MySQL!

This is just a MySQL client talking to our good old Sphinx server. Look at the version in the Server version field: note that it's the Sphinx version tag (and revision ID). And the testrt we're selecting data from isn't a MySQL table either. It's a Sphinx RT index called testrt, defined in the default configuration file.

Now that we've got that sorted out, let's go ahead and populate our index with some data:

```
mysql> insert into testrt (id, title, content, gid)
    -> values (1, 'hello', 'world', 123);
Query OK, 1 row affected (0.01 sec)

mysql> insert into testrt (id, title, content, gid)
    -> values (2, 'hello', 'another hello', 234);
Query OK, 1 row affected (0.00 sec)

mysql> select * from testrt;
+------+--------+------+
| id   | weight | gid  |
+------+--------+------+
|    1 |      1 |  123 |
|    2 |      1 |  234 |
+------+--------+------+
2 rows in set (0.00 sec)

mysql> select * from testrt where match('world');
+------+--------+------+
| id   | weight | gid  |
+------+--------+------+
|    1 |   1643 |  123 |
+------+--------+------+
1 row in set (0.00 sec)
```

The RT index is populated in a different way from a regular index. To make our regular index test1 work, we imported the sample *example.sql* data into MySQL, and told *indexer* to pull that data and build an index. With the RT index testrt, we just connected to *searchd* and put some data into that index directly, skipping the MySQL and *indexer* steps. We used INSERT statements, just like we would use to put data in MySQL. Moreover, we used the MySQL client to send those statements to Sphinx, because Sphinx speaks the same language as the MySQL network protocol. But in Sphinx, unlike in MySQL, SELECT statements did not return the data itself; they returned only document IDs and computed weights. That's because title and content are configured as full-text fields, and Sphinx stores only the full-text index (as described in Chapter 1) and not the original text for full-text fields.

Easy, wasn't it? Of course, to be productive, you'll need a configuration file tied to your data. Let's look inside the sample one and build our own.

Basic Configuration

That *sphinx.conf* configuration file has three major types of sections:

- Data source definitions, which describe where the data to index is stored and how it should be accessed
- Full-text index definitions, which let you fine-tune numerous indexing settings
- Program-wide settings for *indexer* and *searchd*

The following subsections go over the directives in each section that will be important as you start using Sphinx.

Defining Data Sources

As I explained in Chapter 1, the preexisting data that gets batch-indexed into a disk-based index is usually stored either in your SQL database or in XML files, but Sphinx allows other possibilities, too. Data source definitions in *sphinx.conf* tell *indexer* where the data is stored and how to access it. A typical source definition looks like this:

```
source src1
{
    type            = mysql
    sql_host        = localhost
    sql_user        = test
    sql_pass        =
    sql_db          = test
    sql_port        = 9306 # optional, default is 9306

    sql_query       = \
        SELECT id, group_id, UNIX_TIMESTAMP(date_added) date_added, \
            title, content \
        FROM documents

    sql_attr_uint       = group_id
    sql_attr_timestamp  = date_added
}
```

What happened here? First, we defined a source name (src1) and its type (mysql). Second, we provided MySQL access credentials for *indexer* to use when working with this source. Third, using the sql_query directive, we defined a query (the so-called *main fetch query*) that *indexer* will use to actually pull the data. We specified what columns to index as attributes instead of as full-text fields, and what their respective types are. In this case, we want to treat the group ID (an unsigned integer) and the date added (a timestamp) as attributes:

```
sql_attr_uint       = group_id
sql_attr_timestamp  = date_added
```

And that's just enough information for Sphinx to access and index the data.

Additional data source types are also available. Most of them are similar to MySQL but let you access other SQL databases such as PostgreSQL, MS SQL, Oracle, and others. One type is not SQL-based, though. It's called `xmlpipe` and lets you feed *indexer* with specially formatted XML documents instead of having it go to the database for data.

To understand the use of attributes, let's return to the example of book abstracts used in Chapter 1. The book title and the abstract are full-text fields, whereas the price and the year of publication are attributes. Sphinx also requires a unique ID as the first field retrieved in a `SELECT` statement. The configuration options representing these choices could therefore be:

```
sql_query = SELECT id, title, abstract, price, year FROM books
sql_attr_float = price
sql_attr_uint = year
```

We're explicitly declaring two attributes, and everything else will automatically be a full-text field. A thoughtful reader might ask why we don't flag the ID as an attribute. The answer is that *indexer* recognizes it as the first field returned and treats it in a special way internally.

Disk-based indexes

Once you define your data sources, it's time to tell Sphinx how it should index that data. For this, full-text index definitions come into play. Here's a simple sample:

```
index test1
{
    source          = src1
    charset_type    = sbcs
    path            = /usr/local/sphinx/data/test1
}
```

This configuration sets up an index called `test1` that gets the data from source `src1`, expects text data to be in single-byte encoding, and names index files using the */usr/local/sphinx/data/test1.** basename.

You can specify multiple sources and combine the data from them into a single full-text index. This is pretty useful when the database is partitioned (a.k.a. sharded), but the full-text index either is partitioned differently or does not have to be partitioned at all. All the source *schemas*, that is, the sets of fields and attributes, have to match each other to be combined; otherwise, *indexer* will fail with an error. To specify multiple sources, just enumerate them:

```
index test2
{
    source          = src1
    source          = src2
    source          = src3
    charset_type    = sbcs
    path            = /usr/local/sphinx/data/test2
}
```

When indexing test2, data from all three sources in the previous example would be combined into a single index. So long as all the sources have matching schemas, they can vary in location and storage type. For instance, you can pull half the data from a MySQL server on machine A and the other half from a PostgreSQL server on machine B.

The supported character set types are sbcs (meaning Single Byte Character Set) and utf-8. However, any single-byte character set can be supported through the use of another directive, charset_table. This provides a number of options for handling characters: it lets you choose which characters to index, which to replace with whitespace, and how to map the characters to one another (to fold the case, optionally remove the accents, etc.). I will explain this in detail in Chapter 3.

The path directive sets the path for storing files to */usr/local/sphinx/data/test1*, and *indexer* will use that as a prefix to generate index filenames. For instance, attributes will be stored in a plain file named */usr/local/sphinx/data/test1.spa*, and so on.

This example was pretty simple, but in fact, index definitions are quite a bit more powerful, allowing many other options that we did not specify and left at default values. Most of those options control text processing during indexing and searching. You can:

- Choose one or more keyword processors (stemmers, soundex, or metaphone).
- Specify stop words that won't get indexed.
- Specify a dictionary of word forms that will be used to normalize keywords to lemmas (wordforms).
- Create special tokenizing exceptions that override general character set settings and, say, index "C++" as a separate keyword even though "+" is generally not a valid character (exceptions).
- Define special character classes (ignored characters, phrase boundaries, and so-called "blended" characters).
- Strip HTML markup in advanced ways (html_strip).
- Specify substring indexing and searching settings.
- Control various indexing and searching time aspects such as attribute storage strategy (docinfo), fine-tuning options for index data caching (mlock and ondisk_dict), in-place inversion settings (inplace_enable), and so forth. These let you trade off *indexer* disk use for indexing speed.
- Set up distributed indexes.

Some of these options will be explained in detail later, and some are addressed in the bundled documentation.

RT indexes

Another type of index that you can configure is a *real-time (RT) index*. From a usage perspective, it works in the opposite way that a disk-based index works. With a regular disk index, you pull data from a data source (SQL or XML), and batch-index that data. With an RT index, you push data from your application to Sphinx instead.

RT indexes do not use data sources, but Sphinx still needs to know what fields and attributes you are going to use in your index, so you need to indicate these things in your configuration. Here's an example:

```
index rt
{
    type            = rt
    path            = /usr/local/sphinx/data/rt
    rt_field        = title
    rt_field        = content
    rt_attr_uint    = group_id
    rt_attr_timestamp = published
    rt_mem_limit    = 256M
}
```

This example sets up a real-time index called `rt` with two full-text fields, one integer attribute, and one timestamp attribute. There are a few differences compared to regular indexes, namely:

- The RT index type needs to be explicitly specified.
- All full-text fields need to be explicitly specified.
- Attribute declarations start with `rt_attr` instead of `sql_attr`.
- There are no `source` settings.
- There is an RT-index-specific `rt_mem_limit` setting.

The last directive in the configuration, `rt_mem_limit`, is important to get right.

It controls the maximum size of a real-time, in-memory index chunk (RAM chunk) that Sphinx will use for this index. Every change you make to an RT index results in some memory usage, and when *searchd* runs out of this memory limit, it has to store data on disk, and start anew.

Hence, it effectively also controls the size of on-disk RT index parts, and that's the catch. `rt_mem_limit` defaults to 32 MB so that the defaults will be appropriate for smaller boxes. But if you're planning to insert gigabytes of data into your RT index, you definitely don't want it sliced into hundreds of 32 MB pieces. Thus, you need to carefully adjust `rt_mem_limit` with your expected data size in mind.

Sphinx will not use more memory than actually is necessary, so if the RT index only uses 1 MB while the limit is set to 2 GB, it will only consume 1 MB anyway. Optimizing too many small disk chunks, on the other hand, does come with an impact. So it does not hurt much to reasonably overrate this limit, and when in doubt, it's better to specify more than less.

Distributed indexes

Last but not least, Sphinx supports so-called *distributed indexes*. These are essentially just arbitrary lists of any other indexes that you want to search. And *any* means *any*—it can be either a regular or an RT index, residing either on the local machine or on a remote machine, or even be a pointer to another distributed index on a remote machine. Here is an example:

```
index dist1
{
    type  = distributed
    local = archive
    local = rtdelta
    agent = server2.vpn.mycompany.net:9312:archive2
    agent = server3.vpn.mycompany.net:9312:archive3
}
```

Every time we search through dist1, *searchd* will search through two local indexes, archive and rtdelta, make a network connection to two remote servers and search through indexes archive2 and archive3 there respectively, aggregate all the results together, and send the final result to an application. All remote servers (agents) will be queried in parallel so that if every server takes one second, the entire query will also take just one second. Local indexes can be queried in parallel too, with the assistance of the dist_thread directive which we'll discuss later.

Declaring Fields and Attributes in SQL Data

The SQL columns we index are all different. Some of them are text fields to be indexed and searched, some of them are attributes to be stored in an index for later use, and some might not even be real columns, but computed expressions.

Sphinx supports a number of frequently used attribute types, and also several helper features to better index different kinds of text fields typically stored in databases.

For the most part, all columns generated by an sql_query are regular text fields. The main exception is the first column, which is a document ID, and other columns can be explicitly declared as other types. Such declarations let Sphinx know that a column they refer to is not just a mere text field, but either an attribute of a given type or a special kind of field that needs some extra processing besides full-text indexing.

Only a limited number of fields are allowed, subject to technical restrictions. The current index format allows up to 255 fields, but further restrictions in the matching engine limit that to 32.

Supported attribute types are as follows:

*Integer attributes (*sql_attr_uint *directive)*
  Unsigned 32-bit integers. Example:

```
sql_attr_uint = publication_year
```

Bit field attributes (`sql_attr_uint` *directive)*

A special form of the same directive that lets you specify the maximum number of bits that an integer value can take. Examples:

```
sql_attr_uint = forum_id:4
sql_attr_uint = thread_id:28
```

Bit fields are slightly slower to access, but take less RAM. Bit width can range from 1 to 32, inclusive. The different bit fields you declare are concatenated to make 32-bit fields in Sphinx's documents.

So, in the previous example, you would need 32 bits per document to store both forum and thread ID. Without specifying the bit sizes of the fields, you would need 32 bits for each value, which would be 64 bits in total.

Boolean attributes (`sql_attr_bool` *directive)*

Syntax sugar for 1-bit-wide bit fields. Example:

```
sql_attr_bool = is_available
```

Bigint attributes (`sql_attr_bitint` *directive)*

Signed 64-bit integers. Example:

```
sql_attr_bigint = wide_id
```

Timestamp attributes (`sql_attr_timestamp` *directive)*

Unix-standard 32-bit timestamps, equivalent to unsigned 32-bit integers but usable in date- and time-related functions. Example:

```
sql_attr_timestamp = published_ts
```

For timestamps, Sphinx expects a Unix timestamp expressed as an integer value such as 1290375607, not the corresponding "2010-11-22 00:40:07" date and time string. So you need to use `UNIX_TIMESTAMP()` in MySQL or some other conversion function to store the value in your respective database.

Floating-point attributes (`sql_attr_float` *directive)*

IEEE-754 single-precision floating-point values; can store values in absolute range from 1.17e-38 to 3.40e+38, and have six decimal digits or 24 bits of precision. Examples:

```
sql_attr_float = latitude_radians
sql_attr_float = longitude_radians
```

String attributes (`sql_attr_string` *directive)*

Arbitrary text or binary strings, up to 4,194,303 bytes (4 MB minus one byte). Examples:

```
sql_attr_string = author
sql_attr_string = title
```

Multivalued attributes or MVAs (`sql_attr_multi` directive)

Sorted sets consisting of an arbitrary number of unsigned 32-bit integers; can be created from a text field (which you specify as `uint` followed by the name of the field) or a separate query. Examples:

```
sql_attr_multi = uint author_ids from field

sql_attr_multi = uint tags from query; \
                 SELECT id, tag FROM tags

sql_attr_multi = uint tags from ranged-query; \
                 SELECT id, tag FROM tags WHERE id>=$start AND id<=$end; \
                 SELECT MIN(id), MAX(id) FROM tags
```

All attributes with the exception of MVAs are declared in the same way. You use one of the `sql_attr_TYPE` directives and specify the column name.

MVAs are different because you declare more than just an attribute name, and store more than just a single value. There are three different ways to create an MVA:

- Get data from the SQL field, and extract integer values from it.
- Execute a separate SQL query, and use the pairs of document IDs and MVA values that it returns.
- Execute a number of separate "ranged" SQL queries, and use the pairs of document IDs and MVA values that those return.

MVAs are convenient for representing commonly used kinds of 1:M mappings—lists of book authors, product categories, blog post tags, and so on. MVAs are restricted to lists of integers, but this maps directly to a properly normalized database, in which you would have integer primary keys for your authors, categories, and tags anyway. MVAs can then be used for filtering and grouping purposes just like other normal scalar attributes.

SQL data sources also support special field types:

File fields (`sql_file_field` directive)

Uses the SQL column value as a filename, loads the file's contents, and indexes these contents. Example:

```
sql_file_field = filename_column
```

In this example, Sphinx receives `filename_column` data from the SQL database and replaces it with each file's contents. For instance, if the value of `filename_column` is `/storage/123.txt`, that file will get indexed instead of its name.

Field along with a string attribute (`sql_field_string` directive)

Indexes the column as a full-text field and creates a string attribute of the same name, storing the original column value into it. Example:

```
sql_field_string = author
```

Field along with a word-count attribute (`sql_field_str2wordcount` directive)
> Indexes the column as a full-text field and creates an integer attribute of the same name, using it to store the number of keywords indexed. Example:
>
> ```
> sql_field_str2wordcount = title
> ```

Last but not least, there is a special directive that lets you create additional full-text fields from additional queries:

Joined fields (`sql_joined_field` directive)
> Creates a new full-text field by executing the given SQL query and internally concatenating its results. Examples:
>
> ```
> sql_joined_field = authors from query; \
>     SELECT docid, CONCAT(firstname, ' ', lastname) FROM document_authors \
>     ORDER BY docid ASC
>
> sql_joined_field = tags from query; \
>     SELECT docid, tagname FROM tags ORDER BY docid ASC
> ```

Joined fields are essentially an implementation of a kind of indexing-time JOIN performed on the Sphinx side. They are a convenient and more efficient replacement for MySQL's GROUP_CONCAT() functionality.

Sphinx-Wide Settings

The configuration file's sections for *indexer* and *searchd* settings are populated with a number of directives for program-wide maintenance and performance tuning. These directives commonly include a list of interfaces to bind on, log and query logfile locations, various sanity check limits, buffer sizes, and whatnot. Only one setting is required: you need to specify where the *searchd* PID file will reside using the `pid_file` directive. Most installations also tweak *indexer*'s RAM usage limit using the `mem_limit` directive for better indexing performance.

Managing Configurations with Inheritance and Scripting

Configuration files can grow pretty large. Fortunately, two helper tools can help you to keep them concise. First, source and index sections can be inherited, copying all the settings from the parent, and letting you override only the different settings. For instance, it's a good practice to keep SQL access credentials in a separate source section and inherit from it:

```
source base
{
    sql_host = localhost
    sql_user = root
    sql_pass = supersecret
    sql_db = myprojectdatabase
}
```

To inherit from the previous section, refer to it on each source line as follows:

```
source books : base
{
    sql_query = SELECT * FROM books
}

source freshbooks : books
{
    sql_query = SELECT * FROM books WHERE DATE_ADD(added,INTERVAL 1 DAY)<NOW()
}

source authors : base
{
    sql_query = SELECT * FROM authors
}
```

Any inherited value for an option is discarded if the new section specifies a new value. Even if a directive is multivalue—meaning it can be specified multiple times within a single section (e.g., sql_attr_uint in the source section)—the entire list of values is discarded if you specify a new value. For example, the test2 source in the following example will have only the new sql_attr_uint attribute it defines (books_written), not the three values specified in the preceding test1 source:

```
source test1
{
    sql_query = SELECT * FROM books
    sql_attr_uint = year_published
    sql_attr_uint = num_pages
    sql_attr_uint = isbn
}

source test2 : test1
{
    sql_query = SELECT * FROM authors
    sql_attr_uint = books_written
}
```

Second, you can use shebang syntax to script the configuration file. That is, if the configuration file begins with #!/usr/bin/*program*, Sphinx programs will not read it directly, but rather run it through the specified *program* and treat the program output as the configuration file to use.

Once the configuration file is in place, perform the initial *indexer* run to create the index data, then launch the search daemon, and you're all set for searching:

```
$ indexer --all
$ searchd
```

The search daemon can be accessed using a number of different APIs (all providing access to the very same functionality, though), so let's proceed to them.

Accessing searchd

Initially there was only one method to access *searchd*, its native API. This was available natively for a number of languages (PHP, Perl, Python, Ruby, Java, C/C++, C#, Haskell, etc.) and implemented the native Sphinx wire protocol. However, nowadays Sphinx supports a variety of access methods—at the time of this writing, in addition to the native API, there's a MySQL API and a SphinxSE plug-in for MySQL servers, and even more access methods are planned. In other words, your application can submit searches through Sphinx's native API or through MySQL queries. (SphinxSE is an entirely different paradigm.) This section covers the native API and SphinxQL, which uses the MySQL API; SphinxSE is discussed in a separate chapter. We will use PHP for the examples, but the API is consistent across the supported languages, so converting the samples to your language of choice, such as Python or Java, should be straightforward.

Configuring Interfaces

First, let's briefly go back to the configuration file and see how you choose which API to use. A directive called `listen` lets you bind *searchd* to specific TCP interfaces and ports or Unix sockets, and lets you choose the protocol that will be used on that communication channel. Here's a snippet that makes *searchd* talk to the native Sphinx API protocol on port 9312 and the MySQL wire protocol on port 9306:

```
searchd
{
    listen = localhost:9312         # protocol defaults to "sphinx"
    listen = localhost:9306:mysql41 # but we can override it
}
```

By default, *searchd* listens on all interfaces, using TCP port 9312 for SphinxAPI and port 9306 for MySQL connections. The preceding snippet is almost equivalent to the default, but listens on the `localhost` interface only, instead of all interfaces. (This is useful for lifted security in case you only ever need to access Sphinx from within the same server it runs on.)

Using SphinxAPI

From the calling program's point of view, the native API simply provides the `Sphinx Client` class, which in turn provides a number of useful methods. The focal point is, of course, the `Query()` method that does all the searching work:

```
$cl = new SphinxClient();
$result = $cl->Query("this is my query", "myindex");
var_dump($result);
```

Pretty simple. The first argument is the string to search for, and the second is one of the Sphinx indexes specified in the `index` directives of your configuration file. However, just as there are many index options in the configuration, there are many query-time settings. These are controlled by methods you can call on the client object (`$cl` in the preceding example). The client object methods can be classified into these major functional groups:

- Common client functions
- Query settings
- Full-text matching settings
- Match filtering settings (analogous to the `WHERE` clause in SQL)
- Match grouping settings (analogous to `GROUP BY`)
- Match sorting settings (analogous to `ORDER BY`)
- Miscellaneous tools (building snippets, extracting keywords, escaping special query characters, etc.)

Common client functions are something you'd normally expect from any network client API: they let you choose the specific *searchd* instance to talk to, specify timeouts, check for errors and warnings, and so on.

Query and full-text matching settings affect query processing on the *searchd* side. They provide methods to control how many matches will be kept in RAM during query processing and how many will be returned to your program; to forcibly stop the query (and return the results found so far) once it reaches a threshold of found matches or elapsed time; how to weight matches and what per-field weights to use; and to specify what attributes and what expressions should be returned in the result set. And yes, Sphinx supports the calculation of arithmetic expressions.

Query settings are a separate group here, because queries that Sphinx can handle are not necessarily full-text. If you pass an empty string as your text query, Sphinx will basically match all indexed documents, compute the expressions you write, and perform filtering, sorting, and grouping. Queries of this kind are usually referred to as *full scan*, because internally they are indeed implemented using a full scan of the attribute data. They are supported because of public demand: in some cases, a Sphinx query is faster than the equivalent MySQL query, despite the full scan.

Match filtering, sorting, and grouping settings provided by the native API are equivalent to `WHERE`, `ORDER BY`, and `GROUP BY` clauses from regular SQL syntax, and let you filter, order, and group the matches in the result set as needed. For instance, this is how you would search for MySQL books published during the 1990s and order them by price:

```
$cl = new SphinxClient();
$cl->SetFilterRange("year_published", 1990, 1999);
$cl->SetSortMode(SPH_SORT_EXTENDED, "price DESC");
$result = $cl->Query("mysql", "booksindex");
```

The code is rather self-explanatory but shows the general API usage pattern well: you create a client object, set up all the query settings, then fire the query and get the results. Production-quality code should, of course, also add error handling:

```
$cl = new SphinxClient();
$cl->SetFilterRange("year_published", 1990, 1999);
$cl->SetSortMode(SPH_SORT_EXTENDED, "price DESC");
$result = $cl->Query("mysql", "booksindex");
if (!$result)
{
    // oops, there was an error
    DisplayErrorPage($cl->GetLastError());
} else
{
    // everything was good
    DisplaySearchResult($result);
}
```

For the sake of completeness, let's also see how you would group matches by year and compute certain statistics using the native API:

```
$cl = new SphinxClient();
$cl->SetFilterRange("year_published", 1990, 1999);
$cl->SetSortMode(SPH_SORT_EXTENDED, "price DESC");
$cl->SetGroupBy("year_published", SPH_GROUPBY_ATTR);
$cl->SetSelect("*, MIN(price) AS minprice,
    MAX(price) AS maxprice, AVG(price) AS avgprice");
$result = $cl->Query("mysql", "booksindex");
```

You can see that as we add more processing to the query, the code starts to look more and more like SQL. But we build the query from particular pieces rather than express it as a single statement. In fact, sometimes this might be even handier to program than SQL, which often leaves you building the SQL statement string from pieces. However, sometimes it's not so handy, and so Sphinx also provides an SQL interface.

Using SphinxQL

Sphinx's SQL interface actually has two parts. First, *searchd* supports the MySQL wire protocol, meaning that you can use any existing MySQL client to talk to *searchd*. MySQL protocol support can be enabled using the `listen` directive in the configuration file, as shown earlier.

For a start, ye olde command-line MySQL client works nicely:

```
$ mysql -h 127.0.0.1 -P 9306
Welcome to the MySQL monitor.  Commands end with ; or \g.
Your MySQL connection id is 1
Server version: 0.9.9-dev (r1734)

Type 'help;' or '\h' for help. Type '\c' to clear the buffer.

mysql> SELECT * FROM test1 WHERE MATCH('test')
    -> ORDER BY group_id ASC OPTION ranker=bm25;
```

```
+------+--------+----------+------------+
| id   | weight | group_id | date_added |
+------+--------+----------+------------+
|    4 | 1442   |        2 | 1231721236 |
|    2 | 2421   |      123 | 1231721236 |
|    1 | 2421   |      456 | 1231721236 |
+------+--------+----------+------------+
3 rows in set (0.00 sec)
```

Note that in the sample just shown, the *mysqld* server does not have to be actually running or even installed. The protocol implementation is entirely Sphinx-side and does not depend on MySQL in any way. You don't even need MySQL client libraries for this—they enable *indexer* to talk to MySQL, but *searchd* does not use them at all.

Second, queries sent over this wire protocol are expected to be in so-called SphinxQL, which is our own implementation of SQL syntax. SphinxQL aims to be compatible with MySQL where possible, but adds some extensions of its own to make Sphinx-specific features accessible through the SQL interface, too. SELECT statements are almost identical to MySQL, and the grouping example from the previous section can be expressed as follows:

```
SELECT *, MIN(price) AS minprice, MAX(price) AS maxprice, AVG(price) AS avgprice
FROM booksindex
WHERE MATCH('mysql') AND  year_published BETWEEN 1990 AND 1999
GROUP BY year_published
ORDER BY price DESC
```

Supported statements that manipulate data are SELECT, INSERT, REPLACE, and DELETE. Two more statements used on a daily basis are SHOW META and SHOW WARNINGS, which return extra information and a list of warnings associated with the last executed search query, respectively. A number of other statements are supported; refer to the bundled documentation for the complete and most up-to-date list.

The everyday workhorse is, of course, SELECT. It generally mimics regular SQL syntax (in its MySQL dialect), but handles some things differently (it has to) and adds Sphinx-specific extensions. The most important differences follow.

The "table" list
> In regular SQL, a comma-separated list of the tables triggers a join, but the list of full-text indexes in SphinxQL is more like a union: it means that all the listed indexes should be searched and matches should be combined together.

```
/* SphinxQL dialect syntax */
SELECT *
FROM index1, index2, index3
WHERE MATCH('mysql') ORDER BY price DESC

/* Equivalent fully compliant SQL syntax */
SELECT *
FROM ( SELECT * FROM index1
    UNION SELECT * FROM index2
```

```
      UNION SELECT * FROM index3 )
WHERE MATCH('mysql') ORDER BY price DESC
```

Sphinx does not support joins on full-text search results, but does support searches through multiple indexes. So the shorter SphinxQL form improves clarity without conflicting with anything else.

LIMIT *clause*

The difference in LIMIT clause handling is that Sphinx, because of its internal design decisions, *always* enforces some limit on the result set. It defaults to LIMIT 0,20.

OPTION *extension*

This clause lets you control a number of query-time settings that are custom to Sphinx—namely, you can choose a full-text match ranking function; set thresholds for query time and found matches; set a retry count and delay interval for distributed querying; and so on.

WITHIN GROUP ORDER BY *extension*

This clause lets you control which row will be selected to represent the group returned in the result set when using GROUP BY. This is something that regular SQL does not have. A SphinxQL query that groups books by year and returns the most popular book within a given year could look like this:

```
SELECT * FROM books
GROUP BY year_published
ORDER BY year_published DESC
WITHIN GROUP ORDER BY sales_count DESC
```

Finally, native API result sets contain not just matching rows, but also certain meta-information such as elapsed query time on the server side, number of rows found, and per-keyword statistics. These can't be returned with a normal SQL result set, which carries only matches. Using the SQL API, the meta-information can be accessed using the SHOW META statement following the query you want to check:

```
mysql> SELECT * FROM test1 WHERE MATCH('test|one|two');
+------+--------+----------+------------+
| id   | weight | group_id | date_added |
+------+--------+----------+------------+
|    1 |   3563 |      456 | 1231721236 |
|    2 |   2563 |      123 | 1231721236 |
|    4 |   1480 |        2 | 1231721236 |
+------+--------+----------+------------+
3 rows in set (0.01 sec)

mysql> SHOW META;
+---------------+-------+
| Variable_name | Value |
+---------------+-------+
| total         | 3     |
| total_found   | 3     |
| time          | 0.005 |
| keyword[0]    | test  |
| docs[0]       | 3     |
```

```
| hits[0]     | 5     |
| keyword[1]  | one   |
| docs[1]     | 1     |
| hits[1]     | 2     |
| keyword[2]  | two   |
| docs[2]     | 1     |
| hits[2]     | 2     |
+---------------+-------+
12 rows in set (0.00 sec)
```

Building Sphinx from Source

Binary packages aren't always an option. They might not be available for your platform or for a given version, or they might be built with a different set of compile-time options from what you need. We provide this section in case you need to build Sphinx from the source.

Let's begin with a quick-start that takes literally one minute (maybe two) from the tarball to the search results.

Quick Build

For the sake of this primer, we assume that you're installing Sphinx on a Unix variant under a plain account called *sphinx*, and that its home directory is */home/sphinx*. We also assume that a C++ compiler and libraries, the MySQL server, the MySQL development libraries, and a command-line PHP binary are all already installed and ready to use. Enter the following commands, substituting the proper version number for *X.Y.Z* in the file and directory names:

```
$ cd /home/sphinx❶
$ tar xzvf sphinx-X.Y.Z.tar.gz❶
$ cd sphinx-X.Y.Z❶
$ ./configure --prefix=/home/sphinx❶
$ make install❶
$ cd /home/sphinx/etc❷
$ cp sphinx-min.conf.dist sphinx.conf❷
$ mysql -u root test < example.sql❷
$ cd /home/sphinx/bin❸
$ ./indexer --all❸
$ ./searchd❹
$ cd /home/sphinx/sphinx-X.Y.Z❺
$ php test.php -i test1 test❺
```

❶ Configure and install Sphinx.

❷ Create a configuration file by copying it from the bundled sample and imported sample data into MySQL.

❸ Perform initial indexing.

❹ Launch the search daemon.

❺ Use the sample PHP program (which in turn uses the PHP API) to perform an actual search.

If all the requirements were met and everything went well, the last line should print some search results.

Now let's give all the steps (installation, configuration, and API usage) a somewhat closer look!

Source Build Requirements

Generally, any reasonably modern system with a reasonably modern C++ compiler and *make* program should suffice, and there are no other *strict* requirements. Systems that are known to work include various versions of Linux, Windows, FreeBSD, NetBSD, Solaris, Mac OS, and AIX. The minimum version of GCC compiler that is tested for compatibility on a regular basis is 3.4.6. Older versions of GCC might still work.

Sphinx requires a C++ compiler, not just a plain C compiler. It should be straightforward to install one from your OS binary packages. Typical package names for the GNU C++ compiler can be *g++*, *gcc-c++*, *c++*, and so on. You will also need a standard C++ library, which sometimes does not get automatically installed. Specific package names for the Red Hat/Fedora/CentOS family are *gcc-c++*, *libstdc++*, and *libstdc++-devel*. Specific names for the Ubuntu/Debian family are *g++*, *libstdc++6*, and *libstdc++6-dev* (your version ID may vary).

By default, the binaries are built with MySQL support in *indexer*, and thus MySQL client libraries are required. Respective package names are *mysql-devel* on Red Hat, *libmysqlclient15-dev* on Ubuntu, and the like on other systems (*mysql-client*, *libmysql-client*, *mysql-dev*, etc.). However, this requirement can be disabled when configuring the build. In that case, *indexer* will no longer be able to draw data from MySQL. However, you still will be able to use SphinxQL, because *searchd* does not depend on MySQL for that; SphinxQL is an entirely independent implementation.

Note that the server itself is never required; just the client libraries. But for the sake of completeness (and because many sites use Sphinx together with MySQL on the same box), the server package name is *mysql* on Red Hat, and *mysql-server* on Ubuntu.

Configuring Sources and Building Binaries

Sphinx uses the GNU build system. So long as all the required library and header files are installed, the build process is as simple as follows:

```
$ tar xzvf sphinx-X.Y.Z.tar.gz
$ cd sphinx-X.Y.Z
$ ./configure
$ make
$ make install
```

These five commands respectively extract the contents of the source archive (*tar*); change the current directory to the extracted source root directory (*cd*); perform the build configuration (*configure*); build binaries (*make*); and finally, install the binaries and other support files to their proper location (*make install*). Of these, the most interesting stage is the build configuration, because a number of options can be tweaked only during that stage. The most important ones are:

`--prefix`
> Specifies the Sphinx installation root (e.g., `--prefix=/usr/local/sphinx`).

`--with-mysql`
> Specifies where to search for the MySQL client library and header files (useful if auto-detection fails).

`--without-mysql`
> Skips MySQL support.

`--with-pgsql`
> Enables PostgreSQL data source support and optionally specifies where to search for PostgreSQL client library and header files (again, if auto-detection does not automatically find them).

`--enable-id64`
> Enables 64-bit document IDs and word IDs. By default, Sphinx uses 32-bit integers to store document and keyword IDs, generating the latter using the CRC32 hashing function. While that is adequate for smaller collections of documents, on bigger ones, 32-bit document IDs might not be enough to hold the ID values, and 32-bit keyword CRCs can conflict (i.e., the same CRC can be generated for two different words). Using 64-bit IDs alleviates both issues.

`--enable-libstemmer`
> Enables additional stemmers from a third-party *libstemmer* library. Sphinx comes with three built-in stemmers for English, Russian, and Czech languages. The *libstemmer* library (a part of the Snowball project; see *http://snowball.tartarus.org/*) provides stemmers for 13 more languages (Danish, Dutch, Finnish, French, German, Hungarian, Italian, Norwegian, Portuguese, Romanian, Spanish, Swedish, and Turkish).

For instance, the following lines will configure, build, and install Sphinx without MySQL support, with PostgreSQL support using automatically detected client library locations, and with support for 64-bit IDs, placing binaries and support files into default system-wide locations such as */usr/local/bin*:

```
$ ./configure --without-mysql --with-pgsql --enable-id64
$ make
$ make install
```

Once the build and installation succeed, you can use the programs provided by the Sphinx package. The two most important ones are *indexer*, a program that pulls the data from the sources (which you specify in the configuration file) and creates full-text indexes on that data, and *searchd*, a program that runs in the background (a.k.a. a daemon), and handles search queries initiated by other client programs, such as your website scripts. Other programs are:

search

A simple command-line test program that directly queries the indexes (i.e., without talking to *searchd* and therefore without having to run it first)

spelldump

A utility that generates Sphinx-format word form files from ispell or myspell format dictionaries

indextool

A utility that can provide various debugging information about the full-text indexes, check them for consistency, and so forth

All Sphinx programs require a configuration file, called *sphinx.conf* by default, which contains different settings, data source declarations, and full-text index declarations. Two sample configuration files, *sphinx.conf.dist* and *sphinx-min.conf.dist*, are bundled with Sphinx and are installed to */usr/etc*, */usr/local/etc*, or wherever is the default location on your system. They are fully functional, and for a super-quick start you can merely rename one of them to *sphinx.conf*, import *example.sql* (also bundled) into MySQL, and immediately try indexing and querying the test1 index:

```
$ cd /usr/local/etc
$ cp sphinx.conf.dist sphinx.conf
$ indexer test1
$ search -i test1 test one
$ searchd
$ cd ~/sphinx-X.Y.Z/api
$ php test.php -i test1 test one
```

The major difference between the bundled configuration file samples is that *sphinx.conf.dist* lists all the available configuration options along with the default values and short descriptions, aiming to be a quick reference, while *sphinx-min.conf.dist* contains only those few lines that are actually required to index the test index.

CHAPTER 3

Basic Indexing

The preceding chapter should have given you an idea of how Sphinx works in general, how you install it, and how you create simple indexes. But there's much more to indexing and searching. This chapter covers "basic" indexing concepts and techniques that you need to know and use on a daily basis (those days when you're actually working with Sphinx, of course).

Indexing SQL Data

There is usually something more to fetching data to index than just a single SQL SELECT * kind of a query, and Sphinx has a number of features to support that complexity. In real-world environments, you likely need to perform certain maintenance SQL actions at different indexing stages. For performance reasons, on databases that seem to be growing by orders of magnitude these days, you would also want to avoid selecting everything in one go, and instead, divide and conquer. Sphinx SQL sources provide the following kinds of queries to let you do that:

- Main data-fetching query (the only one you are required to have)
- Pre-queries (run before the main query)
- Post-queries (run after main the query)
- Post-index queries (run on indexing completion)
- Ranged queries (a mechanism to run multiple parameterized main queries)

Main Fetch Query

Every SQL data source should be associated with an sql_query directive, which runs the *main data-fetching query* and indexes the database rows it returns. The first column in the query is always interpreted as a document ID, and other columns are interpreted either as text to index (fields) or as data to store as attributes, according to the configuration directives described in Chapter 2.

You can put any valid SQL in your main query. It can be simple, as in `SELECT * FROM table`, or very complicated, using computed expressions, a join over 10 tables, views, stored procedures, subqueries, or anything else that you need and that the database engine supports. Sphinx does not care in the slightest. It just passes the statement to your database verbatim, and indexes the rows it returns. Here's an example that uses seven fields from two tables of the database to produce six fields for Sphinx:

```
sql_query = SELECT b.id, \
        CONCAT(a.firstname, ' ', a.lastname) AS author, \
        b.title, \
        b.abstract, \
        b.year, \
        UNIX_TIMESTAMP(b.changed_date) AS changed_ts
    FROM books b
    LEFT JOIN author a ON a.id=b.author_id
```

Pre-Queries, Post-Queries, and Post-Index Queries

Any actions you need to take before fetching data, such as marking database rows that are to be indexed, specifying the row data encoding to use, and generally performing any other maintenance actions in the database (that your Sphinx instance might require), can be done using *pre-queries*. These are declared using the `sql_query_pre` directive in the data source configuration. There can be multiple `sql_query_pre` statements. They will be executed in the order specified in the configuration file.

Some frequent uses for pre-queries that deserve a mention are:

Enforcing text encoding

With MySQL, the default text data encoding used to send the results to a client application (*indexer* in our case) depends on a number of settings from server-wide defaults to table column defaults, and sometimes leads to unexpected results. Explicitly enforcing a per-session encoding ensures that Sphinx sees the text data in an expected format, such as UTF-8:

```
sql_query_pre = SET NAMES utf8
```

Precomputing various reference values

Indexing might be a lengthy process. Your data may change while it is being indexed, and running the same query at different times might yield different results. For instance, let's say you want to track which rows were indexed and which were not based on their last modification timestamp. If the rows are constantly modified, running `SELECT MAX(last_mod_ts) FROM documents` three times will result in three different values! So you need to compute this timestamp just once, assign it to a session variable (prefaced with @), and use it as a reference value:

```
sql_query_pre = SET @maxts:=(SELECT MAX(last_mod_ts) FROM documents)
sql_query = SELECT * FROM documents WHERE last_mod_ts<=@maxts
sql_query_post = REPLACE INTO sphinx_indexed VALUES ('documents', @maxts)
```

Parameterized queries

Indexes are sometimes almost identical but need to index different chunks of data based on parameter values. For example, a blog search engine might want to keep English, French, Italian, German, and Spanish posts in separate indexes even though those posts are stored in the same SQL table.

In these cases, it's convenient to specify most of the data source settings just once in a base source, reuse the base source through inheritance, and then set query parameters using pre-queries to change the few parts that need to change:

```
source posts_base
{
    sql_query = SELECT * FROM posts WHERE language=@lang
    # many other common settings here
}

source = posts_en
{
    sql_query_pre = SET @lang:='en'
}

source = posts_fr
{
    sql_query_pre = SET @lang:='fr'
}
```

Note that if you need to pick data based on just the document ID range, you should use ranged queries, which we'll discuss later.

In a similar fashion, you can set up actions to take place after indexing using either `sql_query_post` or `sql_query_post_index`. The difference between the two is that *post-queries* are executed when Sphinx is done fetching data, but not yet done building the index, whereas *post-index queries* are executed only after the index was built successfully. An error in building the index will keep the post-index queries from executing.

Pre-queries, the main fetch query, and post-queries will all be run using the same connection to a database. Post-index queries will, however, establish a separate, new connection, because indexing work that happens after fetching the data can be so lengthy that the existing connection will often time out and need to be reestablished anyway. As one important consequence of this, you can freely set and use session variables through pre/post/main queries, but you will need to persist variable values into a database somehow if you intend to use them in your post-index queries.

How the Various SQL Queries Work Together

Let's dissect a semipractical example in which all these queries work together.

Assume we have a MySQL table with UTF-8 data that only gets appended to—rows never get deleted or updated; we just insert new rows with ever-growing IDs into the table.

When indexing this table we want to keep track of the last row that was indexed, to know which rows are already indexed and which are not, and then be able to maintain an ancillary delta index with "just the fresh rows" in it. The following directives accomplish this:

```
sql_query_pre        = SET NAMES utf8
sql_query_pre        = SET @maxid:=(SELECT MAX(id) FROM documents)
sql_query            = SELECT * FROM documents WHERE id<=@maxid
sql_query_post       = REPLACE INTO sphinxid VALUES ('documentstmp', @maxid)
sql_query_post_index = DELETE FROM sphinxid WHERE tbl='documents'
sql_query_post_index = UPDATE sphinxid SET table='documents' \
                             WHERE table='documentstmp'
```

These SQL commands compute a current maximum ID in a pre-query, and then use it in our main query for consistency. Without that `WHERE id<=@maxid` clause, concurrent insertions that take place in the MySQL database between the pre-query and main query could result in more data being indexed than we expect.

We use a separate `sphinxid` helper table to keep track of the last indexed row ID. We want to update it only when the index builds with no errors, so we need to use a post-index query for that. However, by the time the post-index query gets executed, Sphinx will use a different database connection, so we store our maximum ID in a temporary row using a post-query when we're done fetching data, and then promote it from temporary to permanent in a post-index query.

Last but not least, an extra pre-query specifies the encoding we want. If that gets out of sync with Sphinx-side index settings, we'll have a problem indexing non-ASCII text.

Ranged Queries for Larger Data Sets

Indexing data using a single `SELECT * FROM` *table* kind of statement is the simplest type of query and it works well with smaller data sets, but it might not work well on a bigger table. For instance, such a query can stall other queries for a long time if they are run against a big MyISAM table in MySQL; or it can consume considerable database server resources to hold a big lock if it is used against an InnoDB table in MySQL; or it can fail completely with PostgreSQL, whose client library firmly believes in pulling the entire SQL result set into client application RAM upfront.

Fear not, as Sphinx comes equipped with a *ranged indexing queries* feature that automatically generates and runs a bunch of "smaller" statements, each pulling only a small chunk of data. Several directives carry out ranged indexing queries. The can opener is `sql_query_range`, which enables ranged indexing and is required to return minimum and maximum document IDs that we want to index. Then there is `sql_range_step`, which specifies an increment in document IDs that Sphinx will perform on each step. (The default, if this directive is omitted, is 1,000 rows on each step.) When ranged indexing is in effect, `sql_query` needs to mention `$start` and `$end` macros that will be automatically replaced with specific values. Finally, `sql_ranged_throttle` lets you have *indexer* issue ranged query steps with a guaranteed minimum delay between them, giving some relief from the load of the queries on your database server.

Let's look at a few examples. Assume that a documents table contains exactly 20,000 rows, numbered from 1 to 20,000 without any gaps. The following setup will have *indexer* issue 20 queries instead of just one, with the first query "step" pulling rows 1 to 1,000, the second "step" pulling rows 1,001 to 2,000, and so on:

```
sql_query_range = SELECT MIN(id), MAX(id) FROM documents
sql_query = SELECT * FROM documents WHERE id BETWEEN $start AND $end
```

Now assume that we still have 20,000 rows, but their IDs are very sparse and range from 1 to 500 million. Oops, we can't use the previous setup anymore! A step of just 1,000 will result in 500,000 queries and will be extremely slow. We can fix this easily by simply bumping the range step to, say, 10 million:

```
sql_query_range = SELECT MIN(id), MAX(id) FROM documents
sql_range_step = 10000000
sql_query = SELECT * FROM documents WHERE id BETWEEN $start AND $end
```

And with that, it starts to perform well again, with only 50 queries to fetch data instead of half a million.

Indexing XML Data

Besides being able to pull data from SQL, Sphinx also provides a built-in interface to index data passed in a customized XML-based format, called xmlpipe2.

Basically, xmlpipe2 requires you to define a collection schema for *indexer* to use, and wrap every document in a `<sphinx:document>` element. It does not put any other restrictions on your XML data.

An example XML stream could look as follows:

```
<?xml version="1.0" encoding="utf-8"?>
<sphinx:docset>

<sphinx:schema>
<sphinx:field name="subject"/>
<sphinx:field name="content"/>
<sphinx:attr name="published" type="timestamp"/>
<sphinx:attr name="author_id" type="int" bits="16" default="1"/>
</sphinx:schema>

<sphinx:document id="1234">
<content>this is the main content <![CDATA[[and this <cdata> entry
must be handled properly by xml parser lib]]></content>
<published>1012325463</published>
<subject>note how field/attr tags can be
in <b class="red">randomized</b> order</subject>
<misc>some undeclared element</misc>
</sphinx:document>
```

```
<sphinx:document id="1235">
<subject>another subject</subject>
<content>here comes another document, and i am given to understand,
that in-document field order must not matter, sir</content>
<published>1012325467</published>
</sphinx:document>

<!-- ... even more sphinx:document entries here ... -->

<sphinx:killlist>
<id>1234</id>
<id>4567</id>
</sphinx:killlist>

</sphinx:docset>
```

The Sphinx-specific XML elements in the example are:

`<sphinx:docset>`
> Encloses the entire XML document collection.

`<sphinx:document>` *entries with attached ID attribute*
> Wraps every document. The immediate children of these tags are the tags that you are indexing and have identified as text fields or attributes in your `<sphinx:schema>` configuration.

`<sphinx:schema>`
> Provides an embedded in-stream schema. You can also choose to specify the schema in the configuration file and omit this.

`<sphinx:killlist>`
> Provides kill-list data. (We will discuss kill-lists in Chapter 5.)

Documents within `<sphinx:document>` elements can be entirely arbitrary, as long as they are well-formed XML. You can use arbitrary text fields and attributes, and they can occur in the document in any order.

There is a sanity limit on maximum field length that defaults to 2 MB. Fields longer than that will be truncated. The maximum can be raised using the `max_xmlpipe2_field` directive in the `indexer` section of *sphinx.conf*.

Unknown tags (which were not declared either as fields or as attributes) will be ignored with a warning. In the preceding example, `<misc>` will be ignored. In addition, all embedded tags and their attributes (such as `<b>` in `<subject>` in the preceding example) will be silently ignored.

Index Schemas for XML Data

Every index has a schema—that is, a list of fields and attributes that are in it. And indexes built from xmlpipe2 data sources are no exception. The schema plays the role for XML data that the `source` and `sql_attr_xxx` directives in Chapter 2 play for data taken from relational databases. We need to know what data we're going to index before we start processing our first document.

You can declare the schema either in *sphinx.conf*, or right in the XML stream. In case you declare it in both places, settings from the stream take precedence.

In the configuration file, use `xmlpipe_attr_xxx` directives to declare attributes. The syntax is entirely equivalent to `sql_attr_xxx` directives but with the `xmlpipe_` prefix instead of `sql_`; so, you use `xmlpipe_attr_uint` to declare integer attributes, `xmlpipe_attr_float` to declare floats, and so on.

Unlike in SQL source, you also need to use the `xmlpipe_field` directive to *explicitly* declare full-text fields. Elements that aren't declared as either an attribute or a field will, by default, be ignored (with a warning message) instead of being indexed. This is to minimize the amount of required preprocessing of documents as you pass them to Sphinx. You don't have to filter the incoming data to remove particular elements that you do not need indexed from your XML data.

In the stream, define the schema using the `<sphinx:schema>` element. It's allowed only as the very first child element in `<sphinx:docset>` so that *indexer* knows the schema by the time it parses the first document. Elements allowed inside the schema are, in turn, `<sphinx:field>` and `<sphinx:attr>`, which map naturally to the `xmlpipe_field` and `xmlpipe_attr_xxx` configuration directives.

XML Encodings

Support for incoming stream encodings depends on whether the *iconv* library (*libiconv*) is installed on the system. xmlpipe2 is parsed using the `libexpat` parser that understands US-ASCII, ISO-8859-1, UTF-8, and a few UTF-16 variants natively. When building from the sources, the Sphinx *configure* script will also check for the presence of *libiconv*, and utilize it to handle other encodings, if available.

XML Encoding Versus Sphinx Index Encoding

Don't confuse XML encoding with Sphinx index encoding. The former is the encoding that your xmlpipe2 stream uses, specified in the `<?xml ... ?>` processing instruction. For example, you might be storing text files in Russian using the Windows-1251 encoding, and indexing those via xmlpipe2. Your XML encoding would then need to be Windows-1251 too.

The latter is the encoding that Sphinx will work with. And when indexing xmlpipe2 sources, it's always UTF-8 (because `libexpat` returns UTF-8 internally).

So, when using xmlpipe2, you must set the character set type to UTF-8 and configure characters to index in UTF-8 encoding, and not the original document encoding. (We will discuss character sets and their types later in this chapter.)

xmlpipe2 Elements Reference

At the time of this writing, XML elements recognized by the xmlpipe2 data source are as follows:

`<sphinx:docset>` *(document collection)*

> Mandatory top-level element. This denotes and contains the xmlpipe2 document set.

`<sphinx:schema>` *(schema declaration)*

> Optional element. This must be the very first child of `<sphinx:docset>`, or not be present at all. It declares the document schema and contains field and attribute declarations. If present, it overrides per-source settings from the configuration file.

`<sphinx:field>` *(full-text field declaration)*

> Optional element, child of `<sphinx:schema>`. It declares a full-text field. Known attributes are:
>
> name
>
> > Specifies the XML element name that will be treated as a full-text field in subsequent documents.
>
> attr
>
> > Specifies whether to also index this field as a string or word count attribute. Possible values are `string` and `wordcount`. Introduced in version 1.10-beta.

`<sphinx:attr>` *(attribute declaration)*

> Optional element, child of `<sphinx:schema>`. It declares an attribute. Known attributes are:
>
> name
>
> > Specifies the element name that should be treated as an attribute in subsequent documents.
>
> type
>
> > Specifies the attribute type. Possible values are `int`, `bigint`, `timestamp`, `str2ordinal`, `bool`, `float`, `multi`, and `string`.
>
> bits
>
> > Specifies the bit size for the `int` attribute type. Valid values are 1 to 32.
>
> default
>
> > Specifies the default value for this attribute that should be used if the attribute's element is not present in the document.

`<sphinx:document>` *(document)*

> Mandatory element, must be a child of `<sphinx:docset>`. It contains arbitrary other elements with field and attribute values to be indexed, as declared either using `<sphinx:field>` and `<sphinx:attr>` elements or in the configuration file. The only known attribute is `id`, which must contain the unique document ID.

`<sphinx:killlist>` *(kill-list container)*

Optional element, child of `<sphinx:docset>`. It contains `id` elements whose contents are document IDs to be put into a kill-list for this index.

Refer to the online documentation for updates to this list.

Working with Character Sets

How does a computer know the letter *A* from the letter *Z*?

That question is somewhat more complicated than it might seem at first glance, as it involves a bunch of different concepts—characters, byte strings, character sets, encodings and their types, code points, glyphs, and so on.

Digital text begins with (or boils down to) a sequence of bytes, called a *byte string*. For instance, these five bytes (in hexadecimal):

```
0x68 0x65 0x6C 0x6C 0x6F
```

are actually a mere "hello" message.

How do we know that 68 hex is a lowercase *h*? Because there's a standard called ASCII that tells us so. It defines that a byte value of 64 (a.k.a. 41 in hex, or 0x41 for brevity) is an uppercase *A*, byte value 104 (0x68) is a lowercase *h*, and so on. This is just one of the common conventions that "everyone" uses.

The ASCII standard, in fact, combines two concepts: a character set and an encoding. First, it defines a list of 128 characters that it knows about: English letters, numbers, common punctuation symbols, and a few other special ones. This list is our *character set*. Second, it attaches a number in the range from 0 to 127 to every given character. For instance, 104 in decimal (0x68 in hex) is attached to a lowercase *h*. This mapping is an *encoding*.

So, a character set is a set of characters that we know about, and encoding is how we map those characters to bytes.

ASCII is a standard that basically everyone uses. A number of *single-byte character sets* (SBCS) and respective encodings that extend ASCII in the second part of a byte range (values 128 to 255) evolved historically. For instance, the ISO-8859-1 standard adds the letter Æ (the Latin capital letter *Ae*) and assigns a byte value of 198 (0xC6) to it. At the same time, the Windows-1251 encoding tells us that value 198 stands for the letter Ж (the Cyrillic capital letter *Zh*). These two encodings are of the same *encoding type*, because they are both single-byte. That is, they use exactly one byte to store every character they know of. But they are different encodings, so the very same value of 198 means totally different characters in them.

With some of the languages, it gets even "better" because there's more than one widespread encoding—for instance, in Russian, the byte value of 198 (0xC6) means the following:

- The letter ф with KOI8-R encoding (used on most Linux systems)
- The letter Ж with Windows-1251 encoding (used in Windows)
- The pseudographic sign ╞ with Windows-866 encoding (used in DOS and in the Windows command line)

But wait, there's more! Having just 256 characters is not enough for everybody. It never really was, especially in Asia, where the Chinese, Japanese, Korean, and Vietnamese languages use a few thousand different ideograms on a daily basis. So, they invented and used—and still use—a number of *double-byte character sets* (DBCS) that—guess what—encode every single "character" using two bytes instead of just one. And there's more than just one possible encoding (Big5, GB2312, etc.).

Combining Russian with Chinese in one text file with SBCS and DBCS is clearly a mission impossible.

Messing with numerous different local character set encodings had to stop somewhere, and so the Unicode Consortium created a global Unicode standard that can really work for everyone.

Unicode (unlike ASCII, ISO-8859-1, Windows-1251, and other schemes just mentioned) finally separates the notion of character set and encoding, by adding the new notion of a *code point*. The character set is still just an über-list of all characters that Unicode knows of and supports. The code point is just a number attached to every specific character in that list. But given that Unicode knows basically every character in every language out there, including a few dead and a few made-up ones, it's a big character set, far out of the 0 to 255 range that a single byte can store. So the Unicode standard also defines a number of different encodings, convenient for different applications—namely, UTF-8, UCS-2, UCS-4, and so on. UTF-8 is by far the most popular one, because it's the most compact, and it's compatible with ASCII when it comes to characters in the 0 to 127 range.

With a handful of different encoding types (SBCS, DBCS, UTF-8, UCS-2, etc.) and about a gazillion different encodings, it is a good idea to keep everything (as in your database, your application, and your Sphinx) working with just one encoding of your choice.

So, in all this excitement, how does Sphinx know the letter *A* from the letter *Z*?

The shocking truth is that it, in fact, does not. There are just way too many encodings, border cases, and customization needs to have a separate predefined configuration to handle every single one of them.

But you do know which encodings your data uses! So Sphinx provides you with flexible tools to work with your data in different encodings the way you need to.

What does Sphinx *need* to know about the character set and encoding that your data and queries are in? It needs to be able to break down data and queries to keywords, and match those keywords, and that is it. And for that, it basically needs to know only a few things about character sets and encodings:

- What encoding type you're working with
- What characters can occur in a keyword
- How you map characters to each other: whether to case-fold *A* to *a*, whether to remove an accent from *ü* and make it a mere *u*, and so on

Enter two configuration directives that drive Sphinx's tokenizer: `charset_type` and `charset_table`. They are specified per-index.

`charset_type` takes two possible values, `sbcs` or `utf-8`. The former enables you to work with any single-byte charset and encoding; the latter works with a Unicode charset encoded in UTF-8. If your data is in DBCS, UCS-2, or anything else, you can convert it to UTF-8 when passing it to Sphinx.

`charset_table` defines a huge character-to-character mapping table. Every source character in it will be replaced with a destination character and then indexed. Every character not found in the table will be considered a keyword separator. You can think of it as a huge table that has a mapping for each and every one of the more than 100,000 characters in Unicode. By default, every character maps to 0, which means it should be treated as a separator. Once mentioned in the table, the character is mapped to some other character (most frequently, either to itself or to a lowercase letter), and is treated as a valid part of a keyword.

Default tables index English letters, digits, underscores, and Russian letters. (For the careful reader, the SBCS table supports both Windows-1251 and KOI8-R encodings, which is possible because, in this particular case, even though encodings are different, their letter case mapping tables are almost identical.)

You can (and probably should) define a specific `charset_table` based on your target language and requirements for handling special characters. You want to index a percent sign (%) as a valid character, but treat an underscore (_) as a separator? Tweak the table. You want to index Latin letters with accents as is? Tweak the table. Remove the accents from some of them? Again, do it through the table.

The value format is a comma-separated list of mappings. There are a few different allowed forms of mapping. The two simplest mappings declare a character as valid, and map a single character to another single character, respectively. But specifying the whole table in such a form would result in bloated and barely manageable specifications. So, there are several syntax shortcuts that let you map ranges of characters at once. The complete list is as follows:

A->a

> Single character mapping. Declares the source char `A` as allowed to occur within keywords and maps it to destination char `a` (but does *not* declare `a` as allowed).

`A..Z->a..z`

Range mapping. Declares all characters in the source range as allowed and maps them to the destination range. Does *not* declare the destination range as allowed. Also checks the ranges' lengths (the lengths must be equal).

`a`

Stray character mapping. Declares a character as allowed and maps it to itself. Equivalent to `a->a` single-character mapping.

`a..z`

Stray range mapping. Declares all characters in the range as allowed and maps them to themselves. Equivalent to `a..z->a..z` range mapping.

`A..Z/2`

Checkerboard range map. Maps every pair of chars to the second char. More formally, declares odd characters in the range as allowed and maps them to the following even ones; also declares even characters as allowed and maps them to themselves. For instance, `A..Z/2` is equivalent to `A->B, B->B, C->D, D->D, ..., Y->Z, Z->Z`. This mapping shortcut is helpful for a number of Unicode blocks where uppercase and lowercase letters go in an interleaved order instead of contiguous chunks (e.g., accented Latin characters in the U+100 to U+12F range).

Control characters with codes from 0 to 31 are always treated as separators. Characters with codes 32 to 127, that is, 7-bit ASCII characters, can be used in the mappings as they are. To avoid configuration file encoding issues, 8-bit ASCII characters and Unicode characters must be specified in U+*xxx* form, where *xxx* is the hexadecimal code point number. This form can also be used for 7-bit ASCII characters to encode special characters: for example, use U+20 to encode a space, U+2E to encode a dot, and U+2C to encode a comma.

You can find sample tables for different languages and tasks on the Sphinx website in the community wiki.

Sphinx never does any encoding detection or conversions on itself. It always works with the exact raw data that you provide. So, when working with non-ASCII characters, it's essential to make sure all the data and queries Sphinx sees are in the same encoding, and that encoding corroborates with index settings. A checklist follows:

- Is the data coming from the database to *indexer* in the right encoding?
- For instance, MySQL's default result set encoding might be different from the one you're storing your data in, resulting in garbled data sent to *indexer*. Using `SET NAMES utf8` (or what have you) in a pre-query ensures that MySQL uses the encoding you use.
- Is the index configured to use the right `charset_type` and `charset_table`? Are you actually declaring the characters you need to index as indexable?
- Are the queries sent to *searchd* in the right encoding?

Character set settings are embedded into the index and applied to queries against this index. So, when you change `charset_type` and `charset_table`, you need to rebuild the index before they take effect.

To summarize, Sphinx supports SBCS and UTF-8 encodings, and lets you very flexibly configure how to handle characters. You can do case-sensitive or case-insensitive searching, retain or remove accents from letters, choose to index or ignore groups of national characters, and so on.

As a fun fact—completely impractical, of course—if your data is encrypted using a simple substitution cipher such as ROT13, you can decrypt it when indexing. The only problem is that your search queries will have to be encrypted first, because Sphinx decrypts queries using the same settings as when querying the database.

Handling Stop Words and Short Words

All keywords are not created equal, and in your average English text corpus, there will be a great deal more instances of "the" than, say, "ostentatious" or "scarcity." Full-text search engines, Sphinx included, do a good deal of keyword crunching. And so the differences in their frequencies affect both performance and relevance.

Stop words are keywords that occur so frequently that you choose to ignore them, both when indexing and when searching. They are noise keywords, in a sense.

Removing only a few stop words can improve indexing time and index size considerably. In Table 3-1, we benchmarked the same 100,000-document index with varying numbers of the top *N* most frequent words stopped.

Table 3-1. Indexing size and time with different stop word settings

N	Elapsed time		Index size	
	Seconds	Percent	Millions of bytes	Percent
0 (no stop words)	12.2	100.0	73.6	100.0
10	11.1	90.9	67.2	91.3
20	10.5	86.0	63.8	86.6
30	10.4	85.2	61.4	83.4
100	9.6	78.6	51.8	70.3

As you can see, removing just the 10 most frequent words resulted in about a 10 percent improvement both to index size and indexing time. Stopping 100 of them improved indexing time by more than 20 percent and index size by almost 30 percent. That is pretty nice.

Sphinx lets you configure a file with a list of stop words on a per-index basis, using the `stopwords` directive in *sphinx.conf*:

```
index test1
{
    path      = /var/lib/sphinx/data/test1
    source    = src1
    stopwords = /var/lib/sphinx/stopwords.txt
}
```

That *stopwords.txt* file should be a mere text document. It will be loaded and broken into keywords according to general index settings (i.e., using any delimiters that mark the boundaries between words in your text input), and from there, keywords mentioned in it will be ignored when working with the test1 index.

How do you know what keywords to put there? You can either use a list of the most common words for your language of choice, or generate a list based on your own data. To do the latter, perform a dry run of *indexer* in stop words list generation mode, without actually creating an index. This mode is triggered by these two switches:

--buildstops *output.txt N*
:   Tells *indexer* to process the data sources, collect the *N* most frequent words, and store the resultant list in the *output.txt* file (one word per line)

--buildfreqs
:   Tells *indexer* to also put word frequencies into the *output.txt* file

When you specify the --buildstops switch, the output file will be in the exact format needed by the stopwords directive. With --buildfreqs, you will also get occurrence counts. The output in that case is not directly usable, but helps you decide what to stop. For instance, running indexer --buildstops out.txt 10 --buildfreqs on our test 100,000-document collection produced the following:

```
i 740220
the 460421
and 429831
to 429830
a 371786
it 226381
of 218161
you 217176
my 188783
that 187490
```

Picking the right keywords to stop is always a question of balance between performance and requirements. In extreme cases, the latter might prevent you from having any stop words at all—think of a requirement to search, and find, "to be or not to be" as an exact phrase quote. Unfortunately, using extremely common words did not prevent William Shakespeare from coming up with an extremely famous line. Fortunately, few quotes of interest are built exclusively from infinitives, prepositions, and articles, so stop words can still often be used safely.

Sometimes you also need to stop keywords based simply on length. Even enumerating all single-character words can be cumbersome, not to mention double-character words and more, so there's a special feature for that. The `min_word_len` directive in the index definition specifies a minimum keyword length to be indexed—keywords shorter than this limit will not be indexed.

```
index test1
{
    path        = /var/lib/sphinx/data/test1
    source      = src1
    min_word_len = 3
}
```

Given this example, "I" and "am" will not be indexed, but "you" will. Such skipped words, referred to as *overshort words*, are handled exactly like stop words—that is, they're ignored.

However, by default, they are not ignored completely. Even though Sphinx will throw them away both when indexing and when searching, it still adjusts the adjacent keyword positions respectively, affecting searches. Assume, for example, that "in" and "the" are stop words. Searches for **"Microsoft Office"** and **"Microsoft in the office"** will, a bit counterintuitively, return different results.

Why? Because of the assigned keyword positions—both in indexed documents and in search queries. The positions will be different for the two queries. The first query will match only documents in which "Microsoft" occurs exactly before "office", while the second one will match only documents in which there are exactly two other words between "Microsoft" and "office". And because we ignore "in" and "the" and thus don't specify which two other keywords we want, a document that contains "Microsoft... very nice office" will also match the second query.

So, in terms of searching, you can think of stop words in queries as placeholders that match any keyword.

That behavior is configurable with the `stopword_step` and `overshort_step` directives. Both are binary options, with an allowable value of 0 or 1. If `stopword_step` is 0, stop words are ignored even in the position counts just discussed. The default is 1, which counts stop words in position counts. Similarly, if `overshort_step` is 0, overshort words are ignored in position counts and the default value of 0 counts them. If you change either of these directives, re-create your index for the changes to take effect.

CHAPTER 4

Basic Searching

Two principal stages of text searching are to specify what text to match, and then to put the result set of matches into the desired shape, which includes filtering, grouping, and ordering. In this chapter, we discuss everything that Sphinx offers to support these goals: legacy matching modes, full-text query syntax, and additional nonfull-text tools for processing result sets.

Matching Modes

In the beginning, there were keywords, and nothing but keywords, and no query syntax was supported, and Sphinx just matched all keywords, and that was good. But even in that innocent antediluvian age, diverse people were asking for various querying patterns, and ranking methods, and we heard them, and thus and so matching modes were cast upon Sphinx. And they were four, and accessible via SphinxAPI and its younger brother, SphinxSE they were.

Nowadays, matching modes are just a legacy. Even the very concept of a "matching mode" is already deprecated internally. But we still have to quickly cover them, as two out of three searching APIs (SphinxAPI and SphinxSE) support them and default to a certain legacy mode for compatibility reasons.

Legacy modes were a predefined combination of (very simple) query parsing rules, query-to-document matching rules, and a specific ranking method (called a *ranker*).

There are four legacy matching modes: ALL, ANY, PHRASE, and BOOLEAN. You could switch between modes using the `SetMatchMode()` call in SphinxAPI. For instance, the following call in PHP sets the PHRASE mode:

```
$client->SetMatchMode ( SPH_MATCH_PHRASE );
```

In ALL, ANY, and PHRASE modes, queries were interpreted as "bags of keywords" and then matched and ranked as specified by the mode. BOOLEAN, in addition, supported the basic Boolean operators (`AND`, `OR`, `NOT`, and parentheses).

ALL

Documents that match all of the keywords are returned. Documents are ranked in the order reflecting how closely the matched words resemble the query (phrase proximity to the query).

ANY

Documents that match any of the keywords are returned. Documents are ranked based on the degree of the phrase proximity to the query, and the number of unique matching documents in every field.

PHRASE

Documents that match the query as an exact phrase are returned. Documents are ranked based on the fields in which the phrase occurs, and their respective user weights.

BOOLEAN

Documents that match a Boolean expression built from keywords, parentheses, and the AND, OR, and NOT operators are returned. Documents are *not* ranked. It was expected that you will sort them based on a criterion other than relevance.

In addition, there's one nonlegacy matching mode:

EXTENDED

Documents that match an expression in Sphinx query syntax are returned. (Query syntax supports keywords, parentheses, Boolean operators, field limits, grouping keywords into phrases, proximity operators, and many more things that we will discuss in detail shortly.) Documents are ranked according to one of the available ranking functions that you can choose on the fly.

There were several problems with the legacy matching modes.

First, they were very limited. There was no way to do anything even slightly fancy, like, say, matching "Barack Obama" as an exact phrase and "senator" and "Illinois" as plain keywords at the same time.

Second, they essentially tightly coupled query syntax and a ranking function. So, for instance, when using the ALL mode, you could not ask Sphinx to just apply lightweight ranking and skip keyword positions for speed. In that mode, Sphinx always computes a rather expensive proximity rank. Or the other way around, if you liked the ranking that ANY yielded, you couldn't get it while matching all words or matching a phrase, on the grounds that the ANY ranking function was nailed onto its matching mode with nine-inch titanium nails.

Third, once we introduced query syntax support, all the matching modes became just limited, particular subcases of that generic, all-encompassing syntax. That's the course of progress and redundancy in the modern world. The milkman's lot isn't as sought after as it once was...

Last but not least, Sphinx used to have a different code path internally for every matching mode, and that was of little help when maintaining and improving it.

The EXTENDED mode fixes all of this. It decouples query syntax from ranking; you can choose a ranking function separately (using either the SetRankingMode() API call or the OPTION ranker=XXX SphinxQL clause). And adding new full-text querying features does not involve a new "matching mode" anymore; you just change your queries.

So, in version 0.9.9, we internally switched everything to use a unified matching engine, formerly exposed only under the EXTENDED matching mode. When you use one of the legacy modes, Sphinx internally converts the query to the appropriate new syntax and chooses the appropriate ranker. For instance, the query **one two three** will be internally rewritten as follows:

ALL
> Query: **one two three**
>
> Ranker: PROXIMITY

ANY
> Query: **"one two three"/1**
>
> Ranker: PROXIMITY

PHRASE
> Query: **"one two three"**
>
> Ranker: PROXIMITY

BOOLEAN
> Query: **one two three**
>
> Ranker: NONE

Special characters such as quotes and slashes that are reserved in query syntax will also be escaped in rewritten queries.

For compatibility reasons, SphinxAPI and SphinxSE default to the ALL matching mode, so to use query syntax or fancier new ranking functions, you have to explicitly switch to EXTENDED mode:

```
$client->SetMatchMode ( SPH_MATCH_EXTENDED );
```

The MATCH() operator in SphinxQL always uses EXTENDED mode, so you don't have to do anything there to get query syntax.

Full-Text Query Syntax

Sphinx text query syntax builds upon three major cornerstones:

- Keywords
- Operators
- Modifiers

Keywords are just the words you search for, which are treated as atoms, the most basic query building blocks. The chief magic happens courtesy of *operators* that combine keywords in different ways. Combining keywords with Boolean AND and OR, limiting searching to a given field, and phrase and proximity matching are all operators in Sphinx's book. Operators take keywords (and sometimes other expressions) as their arguments, and transform them into *expressions*. We might refer to those as *full-text expressions* to avoid ambiguity with arithmetic expressions such as 1+2/3. Finally, *modifiers* are attached to keywords, and affect the way keywords match.

Known Operators

At the time of this writing, Sphinx supports the following operators:

Operator AND
> Default implicit operator. Matches when both of its two arguments match. Example (with three keywords and two implicit AND operators between them):
>
> ```
> lettuce bacon tomato
> ```

Operator OR
> Matches when any of its two arguments match. Example:
>
> ```
> one | two
> "gloomy Sunday" | "Scarborough fair"
> ```

Operator NOT
> Matches when the first argument matches, but the second one does not. For compatibility reasons, both ! and - are recognized as NOT. Examples:
>
> ```
> shaken !stirred
> shaken -stirred
> ```

Grouping operator (parentheses)
> Explicitly denotes the argument boundaries. Example:
>
> ```
> (red | green | blue) pixel
> bond -(eurodollar bond)
> ```

Field limit operator

Matches when its entire argument expression matches within a specified field, or a part of a field, or a set of fields. The operator is @ and is followed by the field name (in the most basic version). Examples:

```
@title hello
@title[50] cruel world
@(title,content) one (two | three)
@* match me anywhere
```

Phrase operator

Matches when argument keywords match as an exact phrase. Takes only keywords as arguments. Example:

```
"Richard of York gave battle in vain"
"All your base are belong to us"
```

Keyword proximity operator

Matches when all argument keywords that match are found within a given limited distance. Takes only keywords as arguments. Example:

```
"breakfast Tiffany"~5
"Achilles tortoise"~10
```

Quorum operator

Matches when at least *N* argument keywords match, where *N* is a given threshold. Takes only keywords as arguments. Example:

```
"good fast cheap"/2
"single sane sexy smart"/3
```

Strict order operator (operator BEFORE*)*

Matches when its two arguments not only match, but also occur in exactly the same order as in the operator. Example:

```
ladies << first
north << (east | west)
```

NEAR *operator*

Matches when its two arguments not only match, but also occur within a given limited distance from each other. Example:

```
bill NEAR/5 monica
(red | black) NEAR/5 (hat | coat)
```

SENTENCE *operator*

Matches when its two arguments not only match, but also occur within the same sentence. Takes only keywords and phrases as arguments. Requires the sentence and paragraph indexing feature (the index_sp directive) to be enabled. Example:

```
pizza SENTENCE anchovies
acquisitions SENTENCE "fiscal year"
```

PARAGRAPH *operator*

> Matches when its two arguments not only match, but also occur within the same paragraph. Takes only keywords and phrases as arguments. Requires the sentence and paragraph indexing feature to be enabled. Example:
>
> ```
> light PARAGRAPH darkness
> "harley davidson" PARAGRAPH "marlboro man"
> ```

ZONE *limit operator*

> Matches when its entire argument expression matches within a specified document zone, or a set of zones. Requires the zone indexing feature (the index_zones directive) to be enabled. Example:
>
> ```
> ZONE:h1 john doe
> ZONE:(h1,h2) jane doe
> ```

More operators might be implemented over time, so this list isn't carved in stone, and you should refer to the documentation for the most recent version of Sphinx for updates.

Escaping Special Characters

Query syntax reserves several characters as special operators: parentheses, braces, quotes, vertical pipe, dash, exclamation point, and slash, among others. But sometimes you'll want the query parser to treat them as ordinary characters in keywords. For example, say you want to index tweets and still be able to search for **@sphinxsearch** in them. How do you avoid a conflict with the field limit operator?

The answer is the standard one used in Unix utilities and generally in programming languages: escape the characters using backslashes.

```
@tweetdata \@sphinxsearch rocks
```

In this example, the first @ is a bona fide field operator, whereas the second is treated as a character to search for in the document. (And Sphinx discards the backslash itself.)

But watch out: you have to be careful lest your environment or programming language consumes the escaping character. Depending on what environments your query passes through, you might need extra backslashes. For instance, when you run this in your MySQL client:

```
mysql> SELECT * FROM test1 WHERE MATCH('hey \@sphinxsearch');
```

the MySQL client actually processes the escaping backslash itself, leaving Sphinx to receive the query without the backslash and to think that you wanted to reference a field, resulting in an error:

```
ERROR 1064 (42000): index test1: query error: no field 'sphinxsearch'
found in schema
```

So, you need to have two backslashes, one for the MySQL client and one for Sphinx:

```
mysql> SELECT * FROM test1 WHERE MATCH('hey \\@sphinxsearch');
```

And speaking of programming environments, SphinxAPI provides a special call named EscapeString() that escapes all known special characters. What it does is nothing more than a straightforward string replacement, so you can reimplement it yourself if needed, but notice that the version in SphinxAPI gets continuously updated as more features and special characters are added.

AND and OR Operators and a Notorious Precedence Trap

As you can see, most of the operators allow not just keywords, but also expressions as their arguments. Parentheses can be arbitrarily nested, phrases or quorums can be put into NEAR or BEFORE operators, and so on.

This immediately brings up the question of operator precedence. For instance, is the query (one two | three) going to be interpreted as ((one two) | three) or as (one (two | three))? The correct answer is the latter, because OR has a higher priority than AND. The list of operators in the order of their precedence levels (highest to lowest) is:

1. SENTENCE, PARAGRAPH, phrase, proximity, quorum, parentheses
2. OR
3. NOT
4. BEFORE, NEAR
5. AND

One particularly important implication of this is how OR and AND work together. It's a frequent mistake to have a query such as:

```
turtle doves | French hens | calling birds | golden rings
```

that will, because of higher OR priority, disambiguate to:

```
turtle (doves|French) (hens|calling) (birds|golden) rings
```

Not quite the expected result! We definitely didn't have any "turtle rings" in mind, combined with either "hens" or "calling." The right way to express that query would be to use parentheses and explicitly group word pairs together:

```
(turtle doves) | (French hens) | (calling birds) | (golden rings)
```

Along the same lines:

```
(stray SENTENCE cat|dog)
```

would, in fact, be interpreted as:

```
((stray SENTENCE cat) | dog)
```

In this case, the "stronger" SENTENCE operator wins over the "weaker" OR operator, exactly as the "stronger" OR won over the "weaker" AND in the preceding example. So, to match "stray" in the same sentence with either "cat" or "dog", one would need to use:

```
(stray SENTENCE (cat | dog))
```

NOT Operator

The NOT operator likes company. So much, in fact, that it can't bear being alone, and querying for just **!alone** will result in an error message mentioning that the "query is non-computable." (There are several different flavors of this message, but they all basically mean the same thing.)

A more appropriate (but less readable) name for this operator would be AND NOT, because that's how it actually works. The problem with handling a single-argument NOT *X* is that matching all documents that do not match *X* means matching *all* documents in the first place, then omitting those that do match *X* from the list. And that can be a huge number of documents. Although Sphinx can do this, such queries are most likely the result of human error, so Sphinx chooses to protect you from wasting a lot of server effort matching a gazillion documents by mistake.

In case you want exactly that behavior, there's an easy workaround. Just attach and index a magic keyword to every document, and query for it explicitly:

```
allthedocuments !X
```

Another subtlety is that NOT comes in two flavors. Both the hyphen (-) and the exclamation point (!) can be used as NOT interchangeably. Well, almost. There's a difference in behavior between the two when NOT's special character occurs in the middle of a word. Hyphens sometimes do occur in keywords, whereas exclamation points normally do not. So to follow the principle of least confusion, Sphinx never treats a hyphen within a keyword as an operator. However, it always handles an exclamation point as such.

For example, let's say you're querying for **foo-bar**. Sphinx will treat the hyphen as keyword data. Thus, when the dash is in `charset_table`, Sphinx will simply process this entire query as a single keyword with a dash. And when it is not, it will replace the dash with whitespace, resulting in a query equivalent to **(foo bar)**, with two keywords. On the other hand, **foo!bar** will always be handled as two keywords with a NOT, equivalent to **(foo !bar)**.

Field Limit Operator

The field limit operator is a commonly used operator, because people frequently want to limit their searches to an email subject header, or a forum thread title, or a more complicated set of fields.

The syntax is @*fieldname*—and it was conceived before Twitter. (Well, maybe not before the first public release of Twttr by Odeo, but definitely before everyone and his dog was surprised to discover himself on Twitter by Twitter Inc.). If we could do it over, we might have gone with something that wouldn't conflict with the suddenly popular use of the at sign. Or not.

Formal precedence rules for this operator are rather cumbersome. Luckily, they're very easy to explain informally:

> The field limit operator constrains everything that follows up to either the next field operator or the next right parenthesis.

The operator comes in four different forms:

@*fieldname*
: Simplest form that constrains matching to a single field

@*fieldname*[*n*]
: Where *n* must be an integer, limits matching to the first *n* keywords within a given field

@(*field1,field2,...*)
: Field set form, which limits matching to any of the fields in a comma-separated list

@*
: Resets field matching and removes all limits

But what do I mean by "constrains everything" in the definition? This is perhaps best explained with an example that combines field limits and OR. Consider this query:

```
Holmes | @author Doyle | Watson | Lestrade
```

What will this match? As a matter of fact, it will match documents that either mention "Holmes" anywhere, or mention "Doyle", "Watson", or "Lestrade" in the author field. Thus, the field limit operator affects everything after the field name (or names in field set form), and the only thing that can stop it from doing so is the right parenthesis. So, if our true intent is to ransack data for documents that either were written by Sir Doyle, or mention any of our three illustrious imaginary friends anywhere, but are *not* required to appear to be written by the latter two, it is our understanding that it would be in our best interests to alter the query in one of the following ways, sir:

```
Holmes | (@author Doyle) | Watson | Lestrade
Holmes | @author Doyle | @* Watson | Lestrade
Holmes | Watson | Lestrade | @author Doyle
```

The first variant uses the grouping operator (parentheses) to limit the scope of the field limit operator. The second one resets field matching back to matching all fields. And the last one just puts the field limit operator at the end of the query so that there's nothing left for it to constrain.

Phrase Operator

The phrase operator lets you match exact phrases: verbatim quotes, names of persons and locations, and other word sequences of that ilk. Both the operator and its syntax are de facto standard across modern search systems. The syntax is double quotes that enclose a set of keywords:

```
"to be or not to be"
"Albert Einstein"
"New York"
```

Only keywords are allowed within quote marks, and any special characters are ignored. For instance, **"(red|blue) car"** is equivalent to **"red blue car"**. Neither grouping nor OR (nor any other operator) happens inside the quotes.

The phrase operator works with keyword positions, and any peculiarities that you might experience always boil down to positions of keywords either in the index or in the query. In the previous chapter, we discussed how **"Microsoft Office"** and **"Microsoft in the office"** queries produce different results when "in" and "the" are stop words that do not get indexed but still influence positions. The latter query actually matches **"Microsoft ? ? office"** where any keyword is allowed to appear in place of the ? placeholder. As a reminder, setting the `stopword_step` directive to 0 when indexing makes the two queries equivalent again.

But the phrase operator involves a few more complications, related again to the settings in effect when creating the index.

Sphinx defaults to ignoring the punctuation, flat out: periods, hyphens, question marks, exclamation points, what have you. This means a **"punctuation flat"** query will match the anteceding sentence, because its keywords are adjacent to each other. They are separated with a comma in the text, but that comma gets removed and ignored, and does not affect assigned keyword positions. But there are two indexing-time directives that change that.

First are the `phrase_boundary` and `phrase_boundary_step` directives. They work together to give punctuation some "positional" influence that you can choose. `phrase_boundary` takes, as its value, a list of characters in a format `charset_table` uses, while `phrase_boundary_step` takes a number. Characters specified in `phrase_boundary` incur a position increment as specified in `phrase_boundary_step` when indexing. In hopefully plainer English, it's as though we insert several dummy words every time we notice a phrase boundary (a dot, comma, exclamation point, etc.). After you put common punctuation characters in `phrase_boundary` and rebuild the index, keywords separated by those characters obtain some personal space, and **"punctuation flat"** stops matching the previous paragraph:

```
index test1
{
    # ... other settings here ...
    phrase_boundary      = ., ?, !, U+2C # 2C is a code for comma
```

```
        phrase_boundary_step = 3
}
```

phrase_boundary is very straightforward and merely increments the position counter in the index every time it sees a character, without paying any attention to context. Consequently, a document containing "John D. Doe" gets indexed with that extra position increment between "D" and "Doe".

Second, there is an **index_sp** directive that enables some smarter sentence and paragraph indexing code that properly handles a few exceptions to the "separator is a separator is always a separator" rule when it comes to handling periods. A period will not be considered a boundary in the following situations:

- In the midst of an abbreviation (e.g., "the U.S.A. and Canada")
- At the end of an abbreviation (e.g., "Yoyodine Inc. has existed since 1800")
- After a middle initial (e.g., "John D. Doe")

More empirical rules will likely be added in the future to handle further edge cases, but these three yield surprisingly good results. If nothing else, a **"john d doe"** query starts to deliver a phrase match again with the **index_sp** feature enabled.

Last but not least, phrase matches can never span multiple fields. Full keyword positions are, in fact, composed of a field ID and a position within that field, so a change in field is a major change in overall position. To emulate matching over field boundaries, you would need to concatenate fields when fetching data:

```
sql_query = SELECT id, CONCAT(first_name, ' ', last_name) name ...
            FROM documents
```

Keyword Proximity Operator

The keyword proximity operator matches groups of words that are not necessarily in exactly the specified order, but happen to be in close proximity to each other. The unit for counting proximity is keywords, so everything about keyword positions that we just discussed applies to the proximity operator as well. Truth be told, the original reason for implementing the phrase boundary feature was to emulate sentence-level matching with the proximity operator.

Like phrases, the keyword proximity operator works only on sets of keywords, so its syntax builds upon the phrase syntax and adds a proximity threshold with a tilde:

"Achilles tortoise"~3

This matches if both "Achilles" and "tortoise" appear in the document, and if there are no more than two words between them. For instance, "Achilles catches the tortoise" matches, and so does "Tortoise caught by Achilles". If the proximity threshold is n, the document does *not* match when there are n or more extra words between the matching keywords. The document matches if and only if fewer than n keywords "dilute" the matching span.

Here are some rules regarding proximity matching:

- The order of the keywords within the operator does not impact matching. It can, however, affect ranking; the degree of phrase matching is generally computed using the order of keywords in the query.
- All words—stop words as well as keywords—contribute to the count. For instance, "Achilles never catches the tortoise" has one word too many to match the previous query, because "the" is part of the count even though it's a stop word and is not in the index.
- When more than two words are part of the proximity match, the count applies to *all* words, and not each group of two. For example, **"rock paper scissors"~1** will match any permutation of the three keywords, but will *not* match "rock, paper and scissors." One extra "and" in this document is one filler word too many.

So, the rule of thumb is **~1** allows any permutation of keywords but absolutely no extra words inserted between them, **~2** allows fewer than two extra words between keywords, **~3** allows fewer than three extra words between keywords, and so on.

Quorum Operator

A *quorum* specifies how many keywords must be present in a group to qualify for a match. A quorum looks syntactically similar to the phrase and proximity operators, working like they do with a group of keywords, but unlike them, it does not care about keyword positions in the document. It only requires that "enough" distinct keywords are found there.

The syntax is:

```
"good fast cheap"/2
```

The preceding code matches documents that have at least two out of the three keywords. Documents that have all three keywords, of course, also match. Documents with just one keyword do not match.

Just like the proximity operator, keyword order does not affect matching, but can affect ranking when the ranking function uses phrase proximity as a factor.

A quorum with a threshold of 1 is completely equivalent to an OR of all keywords.

Quorum matching is particularly useful when matching all keywords does not return any results, but matching any of the keywords with an OR can return too many matches and can be too slow. Using a quorum operator with a threshold greater than 1 provides a nice trade-off for that case.

Strict Order (BEFORE) Operator

The strict order operator, also sometimes referred to as the BEFORE operator, works on keyword positions, but does not care how many words come between the specified keywords. It matches when its arguments occur anywhere in a single field, so long as they occur in the order specified.

The syntax is two consecutive less-than signs, and arbitrary subexpressions are allowed as arguments. A single less-than sign would not be recognized as an operator and would be silently ignored:

```
ladies << first
north << (east | west)
```

To match, both arguments must be in the same field. A document that has "north" in the title field and "east" in the content field does *not* match **north << east**, even if the title field preceded the content field in `sql_query` when indexing. (Technically, Sphinx retains the ordering of fields, but taking that into account is rather error-prone.) To match that query, the document needs both "north" and "east" in one field, and in the right order. A document titled "North America and Far East" would match. "To the east of North 19th Street," however, would not.

The precedence of BEFORE is lower than that of OR, just like AND precedence is, so be careful about the same notorious catch:

```
turtle << doves | French << hens | calling << birds
```

The preceding query is, because of the higher precedence of OR, equivalent to:

```
turtle << (doves | French) << (hens | calling) << birds
```

That's obviously not as expected, and you should use parentheses to group the (turtle << doves) parts together. AND, however, has a lower precedence than BEFORE. So the following query:

```
partridge << turtle doves << French hens
```

is perhaps unexpectedly equal to:

```
(partridge << turtle) (doves << French) hens
```

and should be fixed using parentheses or double quotes:

```
partridge << (turtle doves) << (French hens)
partridge << "turtle doves" << "French hens"
```

It might help to think of AND as being like addition, BEFORE like multiplication, and OR like exponentiation. In an expression such as $1+2*3\wedge4$, you raise 3 to the power of 4 first, then multiply that by 2, then finally add 1. Similarly, in a query such as this:

```
one two << three | four
```

you compute the OR first, then plug the result into the BEFORE, and then finally do the AND:

```
(one & (two << (three | four)))
```

NEAR Operator

The NEAR operator is a generalized version of the keyword proximity operator that works with two arguments, which can be arbitrary expressions. (The proximity operator accepts only plain old keywords.)

The syntax is NEAR/*n*, where *n* is an integer representing the maximum distance allowed. The syntax is case-sensitive and space-sensitive, that is, near or Near is recognized as a keyword, and NEAR / 3 (with any whitespace around the slash) is also recognized as a keyword along with extraneous punctuation, but not a valid operator.

Distance is counted in keywords and works exactly as in keyword proximity, that is, NEAR/1 allows any permutation of the arguments but no keywords between them, NEAR/3 allows fewer than three keywords between them, and so on.

Because phrases with multiple words may appear in NEAR, think of *n* as the maximum distance allowed between the end of the leftmost argument's occurrence and the beginning of the rightmost one. So, **"Saturday night" NEAR/3 "Big prizes"** will match "Big prizes given away Saturday night" because there are fewer than three words between the end of "Big prizes" and the beginning of "Saturday night".

Even though NEAR is a generalized version of proximity, we need to note how the two behave differently. Specifically, the query **one NEAR/4 two NEAR/4 three** is *not* equivalent to **"one two three"~4** because of differences in gap handling. Indeed, the first query allows up to three keywords between "one" and "two" and then up to three more between "two" and "three". So a document such as "one x x x two y y y three" matches it. In contrast, the second query just allows up to three filler words between *all* of the matched keywords. The sample document we just considered has six, and thus will not match the second query.

SENTENCE and PARAGRAPH Operators

The SENTENCE and PARAGRAPH operators require the full-text index to be built with sentence and paragraph detection enabled, using the index_sp=1 directive. Paragraph boundaries are detected by the HTML stripper, so they additionally require the html_strip=1 directive. Without the proper indexing options, the resultant index will fail to store sentence or paragraph location information, and these operators will be reduced to an AND.

The syntax is:

```
pizza SENTENCE anchovies
```

SENTENCE and PARAGRAPH must be written in uppercase. Otherwise, they're handled as keywords to search for instead of as query syntax. Our example would match documents in which "pizza" and "anchovies" occur within a sentence.

Operator arguments are limited to individual keywords, phrases, and instances of the same operator. So the following two queries are valid:

```
wall SENTENCE "red right hand"
apples PARAGRAPH oranges PARAGRAPH bananas
```

But these two are not:

```
(red | black) PARAGRAPH tree
apples SENTENCE oranges PARAGRAPH bananas
```

Sentence and paragraph boundaries get detected at indexing time using a number of predefined rules. To catch sentence boundaries, punctuation is processed in the tokenizer using the following rules:

- The question mark (?) and exclamation point (!) always indicate a boundary.
- A dot (.) is usually a boundary, with a few exceptions, which I mentioned earlier when discussing phrase boundaries. A dot is not considered the end of a sentence:
  - —In the midst of an abbreviation, as in "the U.S.A. and Canada"; defined as a single inline dot followed by a capital letter
  - —At the end of an abbreviation, as in "Yoyodine Inc. has existed since 1800"; defined as a single inline dot followed by whitespace and a lowercase letter
  - —After a middle initial, as in "John D. Doe"; defined as a single capital letter with whitespace to the left and a dot and whitespace to the right

Every HTML tag defined as block-level in the standard triggers a paragraph boundary. In HTML 4, those tags are ADDRESS, BLOCKQUOTE, CAPTION, CENTER, DD, DIV, DL, DT, H1, H2, H3, H4, H5, LI, MENU, OL, P, PRE, TABLE, TBODY, TD, TFOOT, TH, THEAD, TR, and UL.

Keyword positions get incremented on a boundary: that is, no keyword shares a position with a boundary. Sphinx then stores boundary positions in the index and uses those at query time to check whether there was a separating position between any keywords.

ZONE Limit Operator

Zone indexing and searching essentially adds support for hierarchical document structure, as opposed to the linear structure imposed by text fields.

Zones exist within fields, and map to HTML or XML markup elements. A zone might be everything between <TITLE> and </TITLE>, or <H1> and </H1>, or any other XML tags. Zones can be nested, as the following XML sample illustrates:

```
<chapter>
<title>Compressing Inverted Files</title>
This chapter discusses a variety of <emphasis>compressions
techniques</emphasis>.
</chapter>
<intermezzo>Text in the middle!</intermezzo>
<chapter>
Another chapter content.
</chapter>
```

Note that it isn't necessary to declare *all* tags as zones. You can choose, say, to index `chapter` and `title` as zones, but not `intermezzo` and `emphasis`.

Zones are named. Valid identifiers are accepted as names, with a limit of 127 bytes per name. Every collection and every document can contain an arbitrary number of different zones, and an arbitrary number of occurrences (spans) of any given zone. Sphinx cares only about the start and end of each span, so they can nest arbitrarily, and, technically, nothing prevents them from overlapping (which is forbidden in valid HTML and XML), as long as all open spans get closed.

You define what tags are to be indexed as zones in the configuration file using the `index_zones` directive. Once indexed, zones can be used to limit matching to specified zones only, just like fields.

Unlike full-text fields, zones can overlap and nest, and are not limited in number. However, thanks to their simple fixed structure, fields map ideally to SQL columns and also are generally much more efficient to process. So, zones complement fields but don't render them obsolete.

Two supported variants of zone limit syntax are:

```
ZONE:h1 only in header
ZONE:(h1,h2) only in header
```

Syntax is case-sensitive and whitespace-sensitive, so `ZONE` must be in uppercase, and spaces are forbidden.

Precisely like searches with fields, searches with zones can be limited to either a single zone or several zones at once, and the `ZONE` operator affects the rest of the query, until either another `ZONE` operator or a closing right parenthesis occurs. The `ZONE` limit operator behavior mimics the field limit operator in syntax as closely as possible.

Searches within a zone match everything in any individual span of that zone, including anything that is in a nested subzone. Consider the example document earlier in this section, indexed with `chapter` and `title` defined as zones. Querying for **ZONE:chapter inverted** matches because even though the most enclosing zone for "inverted" is `title` that keyword is nevertheless enclosed by the parent `chapter` zone as well. Querying for **ZONE:chapter another variety** also matches. Although "another" and "variety" occur in different instances of the `chapter` zone, they both occur in *some* chapter, and therefore match in that query for the `chapter` zone. Finally, querying for **ZONE:chapter middle** does not match because none of the keyword's parent zones are chapters.

Keyword Modifiers

In addition to operators, Sphinx also supports the notion of *keyword modifiers*. Some of the full-text operators (notably phrase, proximity, and quorum) allow only keywords for arguments, and exclude other operators. For instance, parentheses are not allowed within a quorum. Modifiers, however, can appear on keywords everywhere, including within a quorum, a phrase, or a SENTENCE operator. There are three such modifiers:

Exact form modifier (=)
> Matches if the keyword occurs in that exact form, as opposed to matching stems. Requires both stemming and index_exact_words=1 enabled in index settings; has no effect otherwise. Example:
>
> ```
> =runs
> ```

Field start modifier (^)
> Matches if the keyword occurs in the very start of a text field. Example:
>
> ```
> ^hello
> ```

Field end modifier ($)
> Matches if the keyword occurs in the very end of a text field. Example:
>
> ```
> world$
> ```

The exact form modifier comes into play when you run your words through any morphology processing—say, through stemming that replaces a keyword with its root form. By default, a stemmed index does not store the original keywords, so you would also have to explicitly set index_exact_words=1 and rebuild the index to enable the exact form modifier to work. In an index with exact words, querying for **=runs** matches only documents containing that particular word, whereas querying for **runs** without a modifier would still match any form that reduces to the same root, be it "running", "runs", or "run". In a sense, the exact form modifier means "skip search-time stemming for this keyword."

Result Set Contents and Limits

We now know pretty much everything about full-text query syntax, but what exactly is Sphinx going to return from a query?

Sphinx's output is called the *result set*, and it comes in two parts: *matched documents* (a.k.a. *row data*) and *metadata*. Matched documents are indeed just rows from the Sphinx database. These results always include the document ID and weight, and might also include additional attributes stored in the index and expressions computed on the fly. Metadata provides a few extra things of interest about the result set in general—the number of total matches, per-keyword frequency statistics, and so on.

When you send a query to Sphinx using a programming API, the result combines row data and metadata into a single structure. The specific structure used varies depending on the language you're using (an associative array in PHP, Perl, and Python; a struct in pure C; a class in Java; etc.), but the structure of member names and their meanings stay the same across APIs. For instance, a result set dump in PHP looks like this:

```
Array
(
    [error] =>
    [warning] =>
    [status] => 0
    [fields] => Array
        (
            [0] => title
            [1] => content
        )
    [attrs] => Array
        (
            [group_id] => 1
            [date_added] => 2
        )
    [matches] => Array
        (
            [0] => Array
                (
                    [id] => 123
                    [weight] => 201
                    [attrs] => Array
                        (
                            [group_id] => 1
                            [date_added] => 1293982753
                        )
                )
        )
    [total] => 1
    [total_found] => 1
    [time] => 0.002
    [words] => Array
        (
            [test] => Array
                (
                    [docs] => 3
                    [hits] => 5
                )
            [one] => Array
                (
                    [docs] => 1
                    [hits] => 2
                )
        )
)
```

Typically, you would walk through matches and process data from them, as the following PHP pretty-printer snippet does. Don't forget to handle errors, though. Reacting to errors is important.

```
// PHP SphinxAPI specific, return matches as a plain array
// (as opposed to an array indexed with document IDs)
$client->SetArrayResult ( true );

// do query
```

```
$result = $client->Query ( "my test query", "indexname" );

if ( !$result )
{
    // handle errors
    print "ERROR: " . $client->GetLastError();
} else
{
    // query OK, pretty-print the result set
    // begin with general statistics
    $got = count ( $result["matches"] );
    print "Query matched $result[total_found] documents total.\n";
    print "Showing matches 1 to $got of $result[total] accessible.\n";

    // print out matches themselves now
    $n = 1;
    foreach ( $result["matches"] as $match )
    {
        // print number, document ID, and weight
        print "$n. id=$match[id], weight=$match[weight], ";
        $n++;

        // print group_id attribute value
        print "group_id=$match[attrs][group_id]\n";
    }
}
```

We can see quite a number of things in the result besides the match data. Let's cover them:

error
> Error message for this result set. Meaningful only for multiqueries. The standalone Query() API call has a different convention (on error, it returns an empty result set, and the error message will be available through the GetLastError() call).

warning
> Warning message for this result set. Meaningful only for using multiqueries.

status
> *searchd* status code. Can take one of the following constant values:

- SEARCHD_OK, meaning everything went fine
- SEARCHD_ERROR, meaning there was an error processing this query, and no valid result set was returned
- SEARCHD_WARNING, meaning the query completed and a valid result set was returned, but with warnings
- SEARCHD_RETRY, meaning there was a temporary error handling the query, and the client should retry the query later

fields
> A list of full-text fields in the queried index.

attrs

> A list of attributes (columns) returned in this result set, along with their associated type numbers.
>
> This list can be different from the list of attributes stored in the index, because we might choose in our query to have Sphinx not fetch some of the attributes, compute things on the fly and return them as attributes, and so on.
>
> The numbers attached to attribute names, such as 1 and 2 in the sample dump shown earlier, are *attribute type identifiers* taken from the SPH_ATTR_*xxx* family of constants (SPH_ATTR_INTEGER, SPH_ATTR_TIMESTAMP, etc.). They don't have to be sequential, although by coincidence they appear that way in the dump shown.

matches

> A list of matches. Each match has an ID, a weight, and a list of values for the attributes specified in attrs.

total

> The total number of accessible matches. (See the upcoming discussion of totals and limits.)

total_found

> The total number of matches found in the index. (Also discussed shortly.)

time

> Elapsed time, in seconds, with millisecond precision.

words

> Per-keyword statistics. This is a list of keywords extracted from the query, along with the total number of documents that match each keyword (docs) and the total number of keyword occurrences in those documents (hits).

Row data is pretty much covered by attrs and matches. Those are the essentials of the search result. The earlier example contained two attributes, group_id and date_added, and their respective types, which are SPH_ATTR_INTEGER and SPH_ATTR_TIMESTAMP. There is just one match (to keep the example concise), with a document ID of 123, an assigned relevance weight of 201, and some attribute values.

All attributes defined in the index are returned by default. When you only need a few of those, use the SetSelect() API call to specify just the ones you need. It takes a single string argument, whose syntax is identical to an SQL select list clause (i.e., everything between SELECT and FROM). For example:

```
$client->SetSelect ( "author_id, year" );
```

Restricting the attributes to just what you need is useful not only to avoid clutter, but for client-side performance reasons as well. Fetching just 20 rows with 100 redundant attributes per row means unpacking 2,000 extra values and putting them into a result set. And in a slower scripting language such as PHP, Perl, Python, or Ruby, that results in a very noticeable performance impact.

Frequently, either you know the attribute type up front, or your language can dynamically convert between the types, so you just access the attributes and refer to them without further effort. If you need to figure out the type of the attribute dynamically, you can check the attribute type data in `attrs`, enabling you to write a generalized result set handler, or just verify your type assumptions.

Everything else besides attributes and matches is metadata. You can check for errors through the `error`, `warning`, and `status` members of the metadata. The `fields` member is rarely (if ever) used in practice, but is still provided for reference and debugging purposes.

`total` and `total_found` are the trickiest part of the metadata. Formally, `total` is defined as a number of *accessible* matches, that is, matches that you can actually request and receive from *searchd*; and `total_found` is defined as the total number of matches found in the index(es) searched, or in other words, a grand total count of all the matching documents that *searchd* just processed. And neither of these is the number of matches just returned in `matches`.

Consider, for the sake of example, the following (real-world) result set: `total` is 1,000, `total_found` is 36,123, and `matches` only contains 20 entries. How do these numbers corroborate, really? Are they arbitrary? No. But they depend on a couple more options that we've been sort of hiding up our sleeve so far: query *limits*. The limits can be set using the following API call:

```
function SetLimits ( $offset, $limit, $max_matches=0, $cutoff=0 )
```

The limits' defaults come into play here. `offset` and `limit` are the offset into the result set on the *searchd* side and the number of matches to pull from there to the application side, and they default to 0 and 20, respectively. (Think of the `LIMIT offset, limit` clause in MySQL.) Coming up next, `max_matches` is what controls the result set size on the *searchd* side. It defaults to 1,000, meaning *searchd* will keep track of the best 1,000 matches at all times, but never a single match more. `cutoff` is beyond the scope of the current example, but for the sake of completeness, it's a threshold that lets you stop searching once it matches that many matches.

So, here's what happens in the previous example. *searchd* runs the query, and finds and honestly processes 36,123 matches. That is reflected in `total_found`. However, as required by the `max_matches` setting, it only keeps, at most, 1,000 current-best matches in the server-side result set at all times. So, it can't return a match number of 3,000; it just does not have it. This is reflected in `total`. Finally, `offset` and `limit` default to 0 and 20, which is why only 20 rows are returned in `matches` in the client-side result set.

You might be wondering why we even have those defaults—that confusing `max_matches` setting that effectively caps matching at 1,000 matches unless you explicitly bump it, and then an equivalent of `LIMIT 0,20` on top. We have the defaults for performance reasons and to ensure clear memory usage constraints. It's enormously more efficient to work with the top 1,000 matches than to process 10 million matches, keep them all in memory, and then throw them away because the query only wanted to show the first 10 matches on that first search results page. In our choice of a default value of 1,000, we were mimicking Google, which never lets you page past the 1,000th search result. (Sphinx lets you bump that limit easily, though. Just keep in mind that the limit needs to be bumped both in *sphinx.conf* and in the SetLimits() API call. Otherwise, a server-wide constraint will take precedence over the API call.)

When should you bump max_matches and what are the pros and cons of doing so? Our general recommendation is to keep max_matches within the 1,000 to 10,000 range. If you set it much higher (e.g., a range of 100,000 to 1 million matches), not only will this result in an immediate performance impact because Sphinx needs to preinitialize a result set with more matches, but it's also an indication that you are highly likely to be doing something, ahem, suboptimal in your application. Most users only ever need the first few pages of search results, and nobody is ever going to actually sit and page through 1 million results. So there's definitely no need to set max_matches higher than a few thousand when it's a real, live person who'll be consuming the search results. But what if it's not a person, but a computer program that needs to additionally process those search results? In our consulting practice, chances are still high that you can do better than merely raising max_matches through the roof. Result set processing on the Sphinx side, discussed in detail shortly, is sophisticated enough to either fully replace or at least significantly offload application-side processing. To supply you with an exaggerated example, there's absolutely no sense in pulling 100,000 matches that match **ipod** and sorting them on the application side by price, as Sphinx can sort them for you much faster. That being said, there still are viable scenarios in which you do have to pull very many matches. Mostly, those arise from data mining tasks, when Sphinx is essentially only used as a low-level keyword searching tool and complex data processing happens outside of it, in the application. Nevertheless, in many cases Sphinx can do everything you need to that result set. And, even with those bulky data mining tasks just mentioned, you can frequently at least do a rough check or preprocessing pass on the Sphinx side and reduce the number of rows that absolutely have to travel to the application.

Back to simple little things, time is the query time elapsed in Sphinx, with millisecond precision, exactly as logged into the query log. So the sample search earlier took 0.002 seconds (which is actually slow for a trivial search that matches one row, but Sphinx was warming up, the machine was busy swapping a bit, and I needed something other than zero for the example). Note that it does not include the network round-trip time spent to send the query to Sphinx and send the result set back. So, time as measured on the client application may and will vary.

Finally, there are per-keyword statistics in the words member of a result set. We can deduce that our query had two keywords, test and one, and that in our full-text indexed document collection, test occurs five times in three different documents, and one occurs two times but in just one document. That's just general prerecorded statistics for the entire index taken from the dictionary. (And, for reference, you can very quickly extract those without actually doing any searching by using the BuildKeywords() API call.) The numbers of matched occurrences in matched documents only aren't provided for performance reasons.

Keyword statistics are there for fun and profit. It might be fun to display them along with search results. And then it's useful to automatically adjust and rerun queries based on these statistics—say, remove a keyword that matches nothing to prevent a query from matching nothing and making the end user upset. We'll discuss a few of those query rewriting techniques later.

Both results and metadata are, of course, available via SphinxQL as well. Attributes and rows are returned from the query itself:

```
mysql> SELECT * FROM test1 WHERE MATCH ('test one');
+------+--------+----------+------------+
| id   | weight | group_id | date_added |
+------+--------+----------+------------+
|    1 |   3595 |        1 | 1293982753 |
+------+--------+----------+------------+
1 row in set (0.00 sec)
```

The SQL result set naturally contains a list of attributes (columns) and matches data (rows), but can't include the metadata. So, you have to run an additional query to fetch it:

```
mysql> SHOW META;
+---------------+-------+
| Variable_name | Value |
+---------------+-------+
| total         | 1     |
| total_found   | 1     |
| time          | 0.001 |
| keyword[0]    | test  |
| docs[0]       | 3     |
| hits[0]       | 5     |
| keyword[1]    | one   |
| docs[1]       | 1     |
| hits[1]       | 2     |
+---------------+-------+
9 rows in set (0.00 sec)
```

The metadata is kept until the next search query (i.e., SELECT), so you can request it several times as needed. SHOW META itself is thus very quick, but normally results in an extra network round trip, obviously. However, if your MySQL client library allows for multiqueries and multiple result sets, you can send the SELECT and SHOW META in one batch, and eliminate that round trip. Recent enough versions of MySQLi in PHP and DBI in Perl are known to support that.

Searching Multiple Indexes

Under most circumstances, you will at some point need to maintain multiple indexes, but search through all of them simultaneously. The other way around, you'd have to store everything in a single, possibly huge, index. And that can only work well in a scenario with a few very specific conditions—when the document collection does not get updated on a daily basis; when it's OK to utilize a single core for every given search; when you don't need to combine multiple entity types when searching; and so on. Most real-world tasks are different, and you will likely need more frequent index updates (counted in minutes rather than weeks), scaling across multiple cores, and so forth. Both updates and scaling, as well as a few fancier tasks, require that you be able to search through multiple indexes and combine (aggregate) results. So, let's look at how that works.

Searching through multiple indexes can be explicit, when you enumerate several indexes in your query call:

```
$client->Query ( "John Doe", "index1 index2 index3" );
```

Separators in the index list are ignored, so you can use spaces, commas, semicolons, or anything else.

Sphinx will internally query every index independently, create a server-side result set (the top N best matches from each index, where N equals max_matches), and then combine the obtained sets, sort the combined matches once again (to restore the order you requested), and pick the top N best matches from all the indexes. This "combination" phase is, by default, very quick, unless you set max_matches rather high *and* there are many actual matches. Sorting several thousand matches in RAM is pretty quick.

The order of indexes in the query is important, however, because it can affect searching results under certain occasions. That's a nonissue when no rows are shared among indexes, that is, every document ID is unique and only occurs in exactly one index. But when a document ID is *duplicated* and occurs in both result sets—a case that likely would involve different weights and attribute values!—we have to pick a single version of that document. Sphinx picks the "newer" version from the latter index in the list. For instance, if **John Doe** matches document 123 in both index1 and index3, and both matches make it into the respective result sets, the data from index3 wins. Note, however, that when document 123 isn't in the intermediate result set for index3, the final combined result set will still contain data from index1, even if document 123 was actually matched. So, in a sense, matching documents from indexes specified later in the index list replace "older" matches. Therefore, in case of a conflicting duplicate row, you always get a "newer" weight and attribute data in a combined result set.

In made-up pseudo-SQL syntax, this process of eliminating duplicates and combining results can be described as follows:

```
CREATE TEMPORARY TABLE tmp ...

INSERT INTO tmp SELECT * FROM <index1> WHERE <search-condition>
    ORDER BY <order-condition> LIMIT <max-matches>

REPLACE INTO tmp SELECT * FROM <index2> WHERE <search-condition>
    ORDER BY <order-condition> LIMIT <max-matches>
```

```
REPLACE INTO tmp SELECT * FROM <index3> WHERE <search-condition>
    ORDER BY <order-condition> LIMIT <max-matches>
...

SELECT * FROM tmp ORDER BY <order-condition> LIMIT <max-matches>
```

Internal index search order isn't specified. In theory, Sphinx can decide to rearrange actual searches in whatever way it deems necessary. The final result set, however, is deterministic and guaranteed to stay the same.

But what does this have to do with quicker updates, scaling in general, and everyday use? The thing is, when using the disk-based indexing backend, partitioning data into multiple indexes is essentially the way to achieve both goals.

Basically, to speed up indexing updates, you put most of the data in a rarely updated "main" archive index (or index set) that only needs to be reindexed once in a while, and you put the tiny "dynamic" fraction of the data that changes actively into a separate "delta" index that can then be rebuilt (very) frequently. Then you search through both the "main" and "delta" indexes.

As for scaling, searches against a single index are single-threaded, so you have to set up several indexes to take advantage of multiple cores, CPUs, and disks, and you can search through all those indexes in one go just as well.

So, in one way or another, sooner or later you *are* going to divide and conquer and search more than one index in one go and have Sphinx combine the results via the routine we just discussed.

Result Set Processing

Result set processing is among the most powerful of Sphinx's features. Interestingly, it doesn't have anything to do with full-text searching. However, it has everything to do with the searching results format that the application sees.

Despite the advertised power, and inevitable tiny devils hidden in numerous details ensuing from said power, it's still eerily simple to explain. Sphinx supports SELECT. Literally. Almost all of the SQL stuff, with a few Sphinx-specific extensions, too. That's the definition of how Sphinx can process the result set for you. Admittedly, it's too general and rather vague, but in a sense it's complete. Now, for all those details...

Functionality-wise, there are these five cornerstones:

Expressions
> When querying, you can access document attributes, compute arbitrary arithmetic expressions, and use the resultant values for filtering, grouping, or sorting purposes.

Filtering (WHERE clause)
> The result set can be limited to matches that satisfy a certain condition.

Grouping and aggregates (GROUP BY clause)

The result set can be grouped by a given column. That is, a group of rows that shares a common value in any of the columns can be replaced with a single row representing that group.

Sorting (ORDER BY clause)

The result set can be ordered by a given column or a set of columns, in either ascending or descending order.

Miscellaneous querying options (limits, ranking weights, etc.)

These options let you request different slices of the result set, use different ranking functions, early-stop query processing, and so on.

The preceding rules apply to full-text matches. So, on top of core text searching operations, you can also add arbitrary arithmetic, filtering, grouping, aggregate functions (MIN, MAX, AVG, SUM), ordering—pretty much everything SQL allows, and then some.

Expressions

The classic SQL SELECT lets you enumerate columns and calculate things, and so does Sphinx. In SphinxQL, you also use SELECT, as usual:

```
SELECT *, price_usd*1.35 AS price_eur FROM products ...
```

In SphinxAPI, you would have to use a SetSelect() call that takes everything you'd put between SELECT and FROM in SQL:

```
$client->SetSelect ( "*, price_usd*1.35 AS price_eur" );
```

Expressions can use the document ID, weight (relevance value), and attributes as their arguments. The four rules of arithmetic, standard comparison operators, Boolean and bitwise operators, and a few standard mathematical functions are all supported:

- Arithmetic: +, -, *, /
- Comparison: =, <>, >, <, >=, <=
- Boolean: AND, OR, NOT
- Bitwise integer: &, |
- Standard mathematical functions: ABS, CEIL, FLOOR, SIN, COS, LN, LOG2, LOG10, EXP, SQRT, MIN, MAX, POW

Comparison operators are valid in a scalar context (as we don't really have a Boolean one). So, (a>b)+3 is legal syntax that returns 4 when the two attributes are equal, or 3 otherwise. The equality and inequality comparisons (= and <>, respectively) on floats come with a feature that is rather unique to Sphinx. They compare values with a small threshold of 1e-6 (that's approximately how much float precision is actually there when the absolute value is close to one). So, when a is 1e-7 and b is 1e-8, (a=b)+3 will return 4, even though a/b will return 10. This might be inconvenient. On the other hand, sqrt(3)*sqrt(3)=3 returns 1, and without the threshold it would return 0. This might be convenient. So, be careful about that if you're working with extremely small 32-bit float values. (And in case you absolutely need bitwise comparison for those, IF() can help, as we will discuss shortly.)

The result type (and evaluation mode) is automatically deduced based on argument types and operations and can be a signed 32-bit or 64-bit integer, or a 32-bit floating-point value. That's loosely based on how expressions work in the C language. However, Sphinx 32-bit sql_attr_uint attributes are (historically) unsigned integers. When evaluated in 32-bit integer mode, their values will be implicitly converted to signed when the operation works on signed, loosely mimicking C again. Then they will be converted back to unsigned when passing data back to the client. So, you might need to reinterpret them as signed values on the application side. Also, if you're storing 32-bit unsigned integer values that actually utilize the most significant bit (that's values over 2^31-1, or 2147483647) and do not want those to wrap around zero in the calculations, you might need to forcibly convert them to a signed 64-bit type using the BIGINT() function:

```
BIGINT(3123456789)*10
```

There's one more conversion function called SINT() that converts its argument (an unsigned 32-bit integer) to a signed integer, returning a 64-bit value to make sure large values are preserved:

```
SINT(1-2)
```

There's also one sort of "anti-conversion" function. Unlike C (but like SQL), integer division such as 3/5 is forcibly computed in floats (and returns 0.6 instead of the 0 that almost no one but a C programmer would expect). But returning the truncated integer 0 can also sometimes be necessary (to please C guys, if nothing else). So Sphinx supports an IDIV() function that takes two integer arguments and divides them as integers:

```
IDIV(3,5)
IDIV(mytimestamp,86400)
IDIV(mydatecode,1000)
```

Sphinx supports a few more functions that do something beyond fourth grade math, too. Some of them (such as IF(), IN(), and INTERVAL()) are modeled after MySQL and should be familiar to MySQL users, but might come with Sphinx-specific quirks. Other functions, such as GEODIST(), are entirely Sphinx-specific.

IF(cond,iftrue,iffalse)

IF() takes three arguments and returns the second one if the first one is nonzero, or the third one if the first argument is zero. For a floating-point first argument, though, IF(), unlike equality operators, operates through a simple bit comparison instead of using thresholds. So, these two lines will yield different results:

```
IF ( sqrt(3)*sqrt(3)-3<>0, a, b )
IF ( sqrt(3)*sqrt(3)-3, a, b )
```

The first one uses a "thresholded" inequality comparison, which tolerates and eliminates the slight floating-point inequality, hence IF returns a. The second one makes IF itself do the bitwise comparison to zero, and because of limited floating-point precision and round-off errors, the argument isn't exactly zero. So, that IF returns b instead.

IN(expr,val1,val2,...)

IN() takes two or more arguments, and returns either 1 if expr is found in the subsequent list of values, or 0 otherwise. The first argument can be an arbitrary expression, including a multivalue attribute (MVA), but its values must be integer constants. Sphinx presorts the list of constants and does a binary search, so even with a huge list these checks are pretty quick. When the first argument is an MVA, IN will return 1 when any of its values matches.

```
IN(year,2001,2009,1997)
IN(friend_ids_mva,30755,288,27353,19614,29567,3916,23445,5290)
```

IN(expr,@uservar)

Value lists can occasionally grow to be huge (up to millions of values), making sending them to *searchd* on every request a costly overhead—interestingly, (much) more expensive than the filtering itself. Sphinx lets you set a server-global user variable once (via SphinxQL, using SET @uservar=(1,2,3) syntax) and reuse it later. Global variables are shared among different connections but are not saved between *searchd* runs, and their contents will be lost on shutdown.

INTERVAL(expr,point1,point2,...)

This returns the index of the earliest turning point that is less than the expression in the first argument; that is, INTERVAL() returns 0 when expr<point1, returns 1 when point1<=expr<point2, and so on. The turning point values must be in ascending order (point1<point2<...pointN) for the function to work properly. This function is useful for partitioning values into buckets and has a few applications. For instance, creating "facets" for a price bracket becomes trivial:

```
SELECT *, INTERVAL(price,30,100,300,1000) AS pricegroup
GROUP BY pricegroup
```

NOW()

This takes no arguments and returns a Unix timestamp representing the moment the query began to execute. (So, it's a kind of named constant, because it gets calculated only once per query for performance reasons, and doesn't change from row to row.)

BITDOT(intval,val0,val1,...)

This interprets the first integer argument as a bit set, and sums all the arguments where a corresponding bit is 1 in that bit set. (The second argument corresponds to bit 0, the third to bit 1, etc.) For instance, BITDOT(5,a,b,c,d) will return a+c. Any of the function's arguments can be an arbitrary expression, but the first argument must be an integer type. The function, in a sense, is "just" syntax sugar, because theoretically, it could be emulated with bitwise integer operations, resulting in something awkward such as this:

```
((intval&1)*val0+(intval&2)*val1+(intval&4)*val2)+...)
```

BITDOT() can be useful for ranking when combined with a so-called FIELDMASK ranker function (discussed in a later chapter) that creates a bit set of matched fields. Another example is when you have object flags stored as bits and want to attach different weight boosts based on flag presence.

GEODIST(lat1,long1,lat2,long2)

This computes a geosphere distance between the two points defined by their latitudes and longitudes, using the WGS84 model. Coordinates need to be in radians and the resultant distance is in meters. Any of the four input coordinates can be an arbitrary expression, and Sphinx internally optimizes them when any of the coordinate pairs is constant.

Filtering

A very common application requirement is to narrow down search results: for instance, to display books published in the past 10 years, or retrieve friends' blog posts, or list products available in the local neighborhood. With a text-only search engine that does not support storing user attributes and working with them, you would have to fetch all matches out and pick the ones you need in the application. But in all honesty, that's an approach coming from the Land of Slow, south of Inefficient Mountains, just north of Terminally Crawling River. This can be an especially unpleasant realization if it happens as you deploy from testing to production. A query seemingly works A-OK when there's just a fistful of matches, but suddenly there are millions. So, what you really want instead, and what Sphinx lets you easily do, is require the search server to filter the full-text matches based on a condition you specify. Not only does that save on sending gazillions of matches to the application, but it also empowers Sphinx to short-circuit searching as it goes. For one thing, documents that do not satisfy filtering criteria are not relevance-ranked, and relevance ranking is a rather expensive effort. The bottom line is that you should never filter on the application side. Always get the attribute data to Sphinx, and have Sphinx do it.

SphinxAPI exposes the following three calls to perform filtering:

```
function SetFilter ( $attribute, $values, $exclude=false )
function SetFilterRange ( $attribute, $min, $max, $exclude=false )
function SetFilterFloatRange ( $attribute, $min, $max, $exclude=false )
```

The SetFilter() call is the API's primary filtering workhorse. It lets you perform equality or presence checks on integer attributes and MVAs. Specify the name of the attribute (or computed expression) to check in the attribute parameter, an array of reference constant values to check against in values, and an optional exclude flag to tell Sphinx whether to include or exclude matches that pass the check. (By default, the results are included.)

Here are a few specific examples that illustrate different kinds of `SetFilter()` syntax and the equivalent `WHERE` condition syntax in SphinxQL:

```
# equality check
$client->SetFilter ( "year", array(2001) );
SELECT ... WHERE year=2001

# non-equality check
$client->SetFilter ( "year", array(2001), true );
SELECT ... WHERE year<>2001

# in-set presence check
$client->SetFilter ( "year", array(1997,2001,2009) );
SELECT... WHERE year IN (1997,2001,2009)

# in-set absence check
$client->SetFilter ( "year", array(1997,2001,2009), true );
SELECT... WHERE year NOT IN (1997,2001,2009)
```

The other two calls, `SetFilterRange()` and `SetFilterFloatRange()`, let you do comparisons instead of just equality checks. That is, they check whether the attribute value falls in the allowed range (as opposed to occurring in an allowed set of values). They are very similar, the only difference being the expected type of `min` and `max` arguments: `SetFilterRange()` expects only integers (either 32-bit or 64-bit), while `SetFilterFloatRange()` works with floating-point values. (Having two methods instead of one is mostly a host language restriction. If there was a reliable method to tell an integer value from a floating value in each and every popular scripting language in the world that the API is ported to, a separate `SetFilterFloatRange()` method would be redundant.)

The `attribute` parameter is the name of an attribute or an expression again, and `min` and `max` are the allowed boundaries, inclusive. For instance, this is how you would check that a book was published in the 2000s and that its price is $50 or less:

```
$client->SetFilterRange ( "year", 2000, 2009 );
$client->SetFilterFloatRange ( "price_usd", 0, 50 );

SELECT ... WHERE year>=2000 AND year<=2009
    AND price_usd>=0 AND price_usd<=50
```

This example brings us to the question of what happens when you issue multiple `SetFilter()` calls. The answer is that all of them apply. In other words, all filters that you set via the API are ANDed together. There's no way to OR filters.

Also, the filters get appended to any existing set of filters; they never replace previous filters. Therefore, this snippet (taken from real-world buggy code) would effectively never match anything:

```
$client->SetFilter ( "attr", array(1) );
$client->SetFilter ( "attr", array(2) );
```

As the two filters stack up, the snippet is equivalent to `WHERE attr=1 AND attr=2`, and that condition never holds true. If the developers simply intended to check that `attr` equals 2, they should have simply used the second `SetFilter()` call. To check that `attr` equals either 1 or 2, enumerate all values in one call:

```
$client->SetFilter ( "attr", array(1,2) );
```

Enforced ANDing of filters can, at a glance, seem like a showstopper for queries that, say, need to match either top-rated or recent enough books. But, in fact, that's a minor inconvenience at most; you still can do that. Remember that filters can be applied not just to the prerecorded document attributes, but to *expressions* computed on the fly as well. Hence, nothing prevents us from computing a condition expression, and filtering on that:

```
$client->SetSelect ( "rating>=8.0 OR year>=2000 AS mycond" );
$client->SetFilter ( "mycond", array(1) );
```

That's the "official" way to perform complex Boolean filtering via SphinxAPI. In classic SQL, the trick we just used is equivalent to this:

```
SELECT *, rating>=8.0 OR year>=2000 AS mycond
FROM books WHERE mycond=1
```

And that's exactly the syntax SphinxQL currently supports, too. However, it's a bit clunky and pollutes the result set with a redundant `mycond` column that always equals 1. It would be cleaner to simply put the condition in the `WHERE` clause where it belongs:

```
SELECT * FROM books WHERE rating>8.0 OR year>=2000 AS mycond
```

At the time of this writing, that syntax is not supported in SphinxQL, but eventually it will be. In the meantime (or if you are somehow locked to one of the earlier versions) you can always use the "filter on expression" approach shown before.

Going back to range filters, there's another semisubtlety with the API methods that you may have spotted by now. Minimum and maximum range boundaries always come in pairs in API calls, and are inclusive. So, how would one check for a mere `attr>3` condition via SphinxAPI? That depends on the `attr` type. When it's an integer (we're concentrating on integers because such precise boundary conditions don't usually arise in floating-point situations), you can just replace "greater than 3" with "greater than or equal to 4", and attach a redundant "is less than or equal to a maximum value of integer" condition:

```
$client->SetFilterRange ( "attr", 4, 4294967295 );
```

Alternatively, you can go with the "filter on expressions" approach again.

Sorting

An amazingly large number of questions in our current reality have more than just one answer, sometimes very many more, and search queries are no exception. And so—what mischievous little creatures they are!—they can very well return more than just one search result. Therefore, we can pose another question: how are those results to be sorted?

Oops, our very question also has more than one answer. The results of a search for a specific product are, beyond a doubt, to be sorted by price—ideally, shipping and handling and taxes included. Sorting news reports, on the other hand, should at least account for how recent the reports are, and if not, they should just sort by day posted. General web search results need to be sorted by relevance. And so on.

Shipping a million matches from Sphinx to the application does not magically become any less expensive just because we intend to sort them as opposed to filtering them, so Sphinx supports sorting on its side as well. The appropriate SphinxAPI method, dubbed SetSortMode(), comes with a few legacy modes of its own:

```
function SetSortMode ( $mode, $sortby="" )
```

The up-to-date approach to sorting is to use the SPH_SORT_EXTENDED mode and pass the sorting condition in its $sortby argument. That's equivalent to an ORDER BY clause in SphinxQL:

```
$client->SetSortMode ( SPH_SORT_EXTENDED, "year DESC, @weight DESC" );
... ORDER BY year DESC, @weight DESC
```

One can use several attribute or expression names in this sorting condition, following each with a DESC or ASC order specification.

There are also five historic modes that can now be replaced with respective "extended" clauses:

SPH_SORT_RELEVANCE
> The default sorting mode. Sorts by relevance, with the most relevant documents first. Equivalent to:
>
> ```
> ORDER BY @weight DESC, @id ASC
> ```

SPH_SORT_ATTR_DESC
> Sorts by the attribute specified in $sortby, in descending order. Equivalent to:
>
> ```
> ORDER BY $sortby DESC, @id ASC
> ```

SPH_SORT_ATTR_ASC
> Sorts by the attribute specified in $sortby, in ascending order. Equivalent to:
>
> ```
> ORDER BY $sortby ASC, @id ASC
> ```

SPH_SORT_TIME_SEGMENTS
> Sorts by a so-called *time segment* computed from an attribute specified in $sortby and the current time. Equivalent to:
>
> ```
> SELECT *, INTERVAL($sortby, NOW()-90*86400, NOW()-30*86400,
>     NOW()-7*86400, NOW()-86400,  NOW()-3600) AS time_seg
> ...
> ORDER BY time_seg DESC, @weight DESC, @id ASC
> ```

Time segments were introduced to sort documents by a combination of freshness and relevance. They split matched documents into six different buckets, which consisted of documents posted less than one hour ago, one hour to one day ago, one day to one week ago, one week to 30 days ago, 30 days to 90 days ago, and more than 90 days ago. Matches are then sorted by a bucket, and then by relevance within the bucket—so that documents posted in the past hour always rank higher than documents posted last week, but within that hour, day, or week, more relevant documents win.

With the advent of expressions, it's now possible to replace that hardcoded time segment computation with an INTERVAL() call and customize the buckets to your liking.

Just for the sake of completeness, there's a fifth mode, SPH_SORT_EXPR, which lets you sort by a C function hardcoded at build time in *sphinxcustomsort.inl*. That mode was introduced before expressions to leave some room for "easy" customization, but now that runtime expressions are in place, the mode is highly unlikely to yield noticeably better performance, and it is very difficult to maintain, is deprecated, and is going to be removed some day. In short, never use it; always use runtime expressions instead.

And last but not least, on the subject of sorting, do you remember the max_matches setting that controls how many matches *searchd* keeps in memory? It's important to understand that this has *no effect* on sorting. No matter what max_matches is set to, it's guaranteed that the very best match (according to your sorting criteria) will be the number 1; the next best will be the number 2, and so on. So, when you sort by relevance, the most relevant document among the gazillion matched documents is always guaranteed to be number 1 in the result set, no matter whether max_matches is set to just 10, to 20,000, or to a gazillion.

Grouping

The very first thing that springs to mind when talking of grouping, as in SQL's GROUP BY clause, is the different kinds of reports—how many site users registered that year, how many sales we generated each week, the peak login hours throughout the past month, et cetera, ad infinitum. So, support for grouping on the search engine side might, at first glance, seem peculiar.

But a number of search-related tasks require grouping as well. What's the average offer price for "ipod" within a 1-mile, 10-mile, or 100-mile radius? How briskly did people blog about Haiti every day last year? How do you display news entries in clusters centered on the same topic and date? The answers involve grouping "raw" matches by this or that, and just as with filtering and sorting, it's generally much more efficient to have Sphinx process a million matches than drag them outside and work through them.

Grouping via SphinxAPI is provided by the following two calls:

```
function SetGroupBy ( $attr, $func, $groupsort="@groupby desc" )
function SetGroupDistinct ( $attr2 )
```

`SetGroupBy()` tells Sphinx to group rows by a value of a function `$func` taken from an attribute `$attr`, then sort the resultant grouped rows by a `$groupsort` condition. In SphinxQL, it's equivalent to this clause:

```
GROUP BY $func($attribute) ORDER BY $groupsort
```

`SetGroupDistinct()` makes Sphinx count the number of distinct values of attribute `$attr2` while grouping by some other attribute. The equivalent SphinxQL is (you bet) adding `COUNT(DISTINCT $attr2)` to the `SELECT` expressions list.

The calls add a few magic columns to the result set. `SetGroupBy()` adds an `@groupby` column that contains the value used for grouping and an `@count` that contains the number of rows in that group. `SetGroupDistinct()` returns the number of distinct `$attr2` values in a magic `@distinct` column.

Here's what the bundled *test.php* application displays when "just" searching and then when grouping (by a `group_id` attribute):

```
$ php test.php -i test1 test
Query 'test' retrieved 3 of 3 matches in 0.000 sec.
Query stats:
    'test' found 5 times in 3 documents

Matches:
1. doc_id=1, weight=101, group_id=1, date_added=2011-01-02 18:39:13
2. doc_id=2, weight=101, group_id=1, date_added=2011-01-02 18:39:13
3. doc_id=4, weight=1, group_id=2, date_added=2011-01-02 18:39:13

$ php test.php -i test1 -g group_id test
Query 'test' retrieved 2 of 2 matches in 0.000 sec.
Query stats:
    'test' found 5 times in 3 documents

Matches:
1. doc_id=4, weight=1, group_id=2, date_added=2011-01-02 18:39:13,
    @groupby=2, @count=1
2. doc_id=1, weight=101, group_id=1, date_added=2011-01-02 18:39:13,
    @groupby=1, @count=2
```

You can see how, with grouping enabled, we're getting two groups instead of three documents now, along with associated group-by key and counts.

But hey, why aren't the results in ascending relevance (weight) order anymore?

Remember that the `SetGroupBy()` call maps to both `GROUP BY` and `ORDER BY` clauses in SphinxQL. And, by default, it chooses to order the *groups* that now make it into the result set by group-by key. However, the *matches* sorting (the one from the previous section, which can be set with the `SetSortMode()` call and defaults to relevance order), does not get left out either. When grouping is in effect, it's used to pick the one row that will represent the group in the final result set. In SQL terms:

When `SetGroupBy()` *is enabled*, `SetSortMode()` *is equivalent to the* `WITHIN GROUP ORDER BY` *clause in the SphinxQL dialect.*

Otherwise, `SetSortMode()` *is equivalent to the* `ORDER BY` *clause.*

`WITHIN GROUP ORDER BY` is a SphinxQL-specific extension. The SQL standard does not specify what representative row to pick for a group, and does not introduce any syntax to control the choice. So technically, an SQL database can even return a random row every time you repeat the query without breaking the standard. Our extension lets you specify which row to choose. For instance, as the default sorting mode is essentially `@weight DESC, @id ASC`, the most relevant row within each group will be picked by default. (If more than one row has the same top relevance value, the document with a smaller document ID wins. This explains why document 1 was returned in the earlier example.) But you can override that and, say, pick the most recently added row instead:

```
SELECT * FROM test1
GROUP BY group_id
WITHIN GROUP ORDER BY date_added DESC
ORDER BY @weight DESC
```

Unobtrusively switching from SphinxAPI to SphinxQL now, grouping isn't only about removing "duplicate" rows that share a common value in a given column; it's also about computing *aggregate functions* over such groups of row. Two examples we've covered are `COUNT(*)` and `COUNT(DISTINCT attr)`, but Sphinx supports more. Currently, you can use `MIN()`, `MAX()`, `AVG()`, and `SUM()`, which covers the ANSI SQL'92 standard. A few more sophisticated aggregate functions (e.g., bitwise operations, standard deviance and variation, etc.) may be added in the future, so refer to the current documentation for the most recent list.

```
SELECT *, AVG(price) FROM products
WHERE MATCH('ipod')
GROUP BY city_id
```

An important side note is that Sphinx's current implementation of aggregate functions can be intentionally imprecise in favor of performance and constrained RAM use. The degree of precision depends on the value of the `max_matches` option. Sphinx will only keep track of `4*max_matches` best groups (as per sorting criteria) at all times. Thus, when the result set contains fewer than that number of groups the aggregate values are guaranteed to be precise. Otherwise, the values can be (slightly) off.

CHAPTER 5

Managing Indexes

As we briefly mentioned in the preceding chapter, Sphinx lets you search through multiple indexes at the same time. There are usually two reasons for devoting multiple indexes to the same application area: the main+delta strategy that greatly reduces the delay in keeping an index up-to-date, and parallelizing queries across indexes to reduce the delay in responding to queries. All serious production sites use multiple indexes, so you'll find this chapter to be a natural sequel to the preceding one. The strategy leads to complexities that I'll cover in this chapter. But I'll occasionally diverge from the "general overview" approach of previous chapters and focus more on specific features, all of the nitty and even some of the gritty details of engine internals, and concrete use cases and dos and don'ts.

The "Divide and Conquer" Concept

Plain disk indexes need to be fully rebuilt from scratch every time you need to update the text data they contain. This can lead to delays of minutes or even hours before new and updated rows appear in response to queries—and that's not even considering the waste of CPU cycles and networking.

Many people, including myself, lack the patience for this. Should you stand for this in your very own applications? It depends on the numbers, and concrete figures are easy to approximate with a bit of simple back-of-the-envelope math.

On modern commodity gear (which, at the time of this writing, means multicore CPUs clocked at 3.0 GHz, give or take a few hundred megahertz, and SATA or SAS disk drives at 7,200 to 15,000 rpm, yielding 5 to .15 millisecond seeks and 100 MB/second linear transfer speeds), Sphinx indexing usually goes through 6 to 12 MB/second worth of raw text with a single CPU and a single HDD. Actually, the aged desktop I'm using to write this text, with 2 GB of RAM, a 7,200 rpm SATA drive, and a dual-core 3.16 GHz CPU (Core 2 Duo E8500), is able to index at almost 10 MB/second, and that includes fetching data from a cold database. That workload scenario is subtly different from a typical production one, because, unlike in production, my testing database file is defragmented and essentially read-only, and said desktop gets no other load when indexing. But a typical production server is usually beefier to compensate.

So, if you're running an ebusiness and you need to index, say, 300,000 products, with every product row taking less than 1 KB of text, that's less than 300 MB total and, at 10 MB/second, can take as little as 30 seconds to rebuild from scratch. At that scale, you are perfectly fine with a single index that gets rebuilt frequently enough.

On the other hand, 10 million business documents (think memos, reports, etc.) that convert to 20 KB of text (about 10 pages) on average mean 200 GB of data for Sphinx to index. That's a difference of three orders of magnitude. It's still theoretically doable on a single server, inasmuch as 200 GB at 10 MB/second means 20,000 seconds, or roughly 5.5 hours. But you probably want new documents to become searchable much faster than that, and you definitely don't want to spend six hours every day reindexing the very same data over and over again.

Hold everything—I said it was the very same data, but the whole point of reindexing is that documents can surely change over time. Yes, but at that scale the *majority* of the data is unlikely to change at a fast pace. An army of 1,000 qualified typists sustaining a rate of about 400 words per minute each for eight hours a day means "just" over 1 GB of data per day (2.5 KB/minute * 480 minutes * 1,000 typists = 1.2 GB). Does your organization actually employ that many typists, and therefore produce even that much data per day? I am compelled to think not—unless your badge reads "CIA" or your last name is Wolton. So, we can expect that even on a 100 GB to a 1 TB scale, internal data trickles through in mere gigabytes.

Now, gigabytes take minutes to index, whereas terabytes take whole hours, so it's clearly time to divide and conquer.

Let's segregate our data. Naturally, we'll divide it by freshness. Assume, for the sake of argument, that we have a collection of 10 million documents, and an average of 10,000 are added daily. We can keep track of when a document was added via a simple `date_added` column in a database (often filled automatically with the right timestamp), which works like a charm. To start, we put the huge preexisting 10 million-document archive into one big index, and memorize the date we started on the right path. That will be our *main* index; our primary, infrequently updated archive. Tomorrow, instead of rebuilding it and ending up with one big 10,010,000-document index, we pick the 10,000 new documents only, and build a *delta* index that's a thousand times smaller. That, the envelope says, should take about 20 seconds to create. Much better!

We can now rebuild the delta index every minute with ease, and then use both indexes when searching. And ... *voilà!* We've just set up a nifty little instance of the *main+delta scheme* that saves us from a six-hour index rebuild every day.

Formally, with the main+delta scheme the data is put into two or more different indexes of different sizes and is reindexed at different intervals to save the resources spent on indexing data and minimize the indexing lag (i.e., the delay until the document entered into the system can materialize in search results).

Our little example has shown how to quickly add the new documents "tomorrow," but it poses a number of additional questions. We've got tomorrow covered, but what do we do the day after? What about in a week? What if we not only need to add new documents, but delete and edit existing ones as well? Specifically, how can we differentiate new documents from old ones? More importantly, how *should* we? Last but not least, how *exactly* do we handle that rebuild part? Surely we don't want to stop *searchd* while the rebuild is running; but what do we do?

Let's answer those intriguing questions, commencing with having the latest and greatest one for the subject of our next section.

Index Rotation

Index rotation is, basically, how new data gets into *searchd* without disrupting normal search operations.

The Sphinx index is physically just a set of files (sharing the same name but having a few different extensions). *indexer* creates and writes them when indexing, and *searchd* reads them when searching. By default, *indexer* overwrites those files. But that would obviously ruin any search queries that try to execute in the meantime. So, both *searchd* and *indexer* lock all indexes they are currently using. That prevents overwrites in case someone else (either *searchd* or a concurrent *indexer*) is using an index. An attempt to read a locked index produces an error such as the following:

```
$ indexer test1
FATAL: failed to lock /var/data/test1.spl: Resource temporarily
unavailable, will not index. Try --rotate option.
```

Running the search daemon is the most probable cause of the inability to lock the index, so *indexer* suggests rotating the index instead of creating it. (As a side note, the second and third most common causes for the "failed to lock" message are a wrong path or permissions, and a concurrent *indexer*, respectively.)

Giving the --rotate switch informs *indexer* that the target index is busy and must not be overwritten, and indexing veers a bit. A new set of index files gets created under a different name. The current copy of the index files is not touched, so *searchd* can safely use it for searching in the meantime. Once the indexing completes successfully, *indexer* sends a SIGHUP signal to *searchd*. That's how the search daemon knows it's time to pick up a new version (or versions) of the index. If *searchd* succeeds in loading a new index version, the daemon renames the current index files as old, renames the new ones as current, and works queries off the new versions from that moment on. If not, it logs an error and keeps using the current good version.

"Current" index filenames are constructed from the path directive in the configuration files index settings by appending a few different extensions, all falling under the *.sp** wildcard. "New" versions get *.new.sp** extensions and "old" versions get *.old.sp.** extensions. So, a bit more specifically, the rotation process works as follows:

1. *indexer* builds *.new.sp** files.
2. *indexer* sends SIGHUP to *searchd*.
3. *searchd* checks all active indexes looking for *.new.sp** files.
4. For every index, it tries to load *.new.sp**.
5. On error, it logs that in *searchd.log*.
6. On success, it renames the current *.sp** as *.old.sp**, and *.new.sp** as *.sp**.
7. When `unlink_old=1` is set, *searchd* also unlinks *.old.sp**.

A careful reader might notice that an error can occur during renaming as well, not just when loading a new version. This isn't a hypothetical situation. For instance, if there already are conflicting *.old* files with wrong permissions, renaming current files would fail miserably. That is also handled as an error, and Sphinx falls back to using the current version of the index in this case as well, rolling back all renames it made so far. (For the really picky reader, failures during rollback are also handled, but not very gracefully, as we never saw a single one actually happen. So those still are purely theoretical fiends.)

Back to a more significant question, what is "loading" of the index really about and when does "unloading" of the old index occur? We need to point out that *searchd* keeps some of the index files precached in memory at all times, for performance reasons: document attributes, the kill-list (discussed later), and the dictionary data are kept. So, "loading" means bringing those into RAM, and "unloading" means freeing that RAM. Normally, we don't want any interruptions to the querying that happens in the meantime, so by default, *searchd* loads new data, then switches incoming queries to use the new index, then waits for queries working with old data to complete, and only then unloads old data. That's called *seamless rotation*. However, that means 2x spikes in RAM use during rotation, which might be a problem.

Nonseamless rotation, enabled with the `seamless_rotate=0` directive, can be used to alleviate this burden. When it takes place, *searchd* waits for pending queries to complete first, then unloads old data, and only then loads new data. Queries (to a rotated index) that arrive in the meantime are rejected with a "temporary error" status. So you essentially have a choice between whatever you consider to be the lesser of two evils, as there have to be either RAM usage spikes or temporary query failures during rotation.

Rotation is performed not only on SIGHUP, but on startup as well. So, if you've built a shadow copy with `indexer --rotate` while the search daemon was not running (and a SIGHUP shot that *indexer* made totally missed the mark), just start *searchd* and it should pick up a proper, new copy of the index anyway.

By default, *indexer* will send a SIGHUP just once per invocation, in the end, when it's done building everything it was asked to build. This is convenient when you're rebuilding many small indexes, and not quite so when you're rebuilding a few big data chunks. So, there's a `--sighup-each` command-line switch that makes *indexer* send a SIGHUP after each index.

Picking Documents

It has been brought to my attention that we're far outta the runway and long airborne over the land of split indexes, main+delta schemes, and rotation and we haven't seen a single working example. That is starkly inadmissible and requires immediate intervention.

Let's go back to that example when we only insert new documents into the database, without updating or deleting any documents. Let's assume (for now) that they reside in a MySQL table called `documents` that has an ever-growing auto-increment primary key named `ID`.

To differentiate between "old" and "new" documents, we need to store a border value for every index. The last maximum indexed document ID works fine here. So, our first step is to create a helper table that stores it:

```
CREATE TABLE sphinxcounters (
    tablename VARCHAR(255) NOT NULL PRIMARY KEY,
    maxid BIGINT NOT NULL );
```

The data source for the main index now needs to update `sphinxcounters` so that the data source for the delta index can fetch the rows added since the last main index rebuild. How would you configure that main source? Chances are good that a first try would look something like this:

```
source srcmain
{
    type          = mysql
    sql_host      = localhost
    sql_user      = root
    sql_pass      =
    sql_db        = test
    sql_query     = SELECT * FROM documents
    sql_query_post = REPLACE INTO sphinxcounters \
        SELECT 'documents',  MAX(id) FROM documents
}
```

Unfortunately, while this is very simple and seems to work, it's also wrong, for a few different reasons.

First problem: what happens if indexing fails *after* a post-query updates a helper `sphinxcounters` table? Subsequent delta index rebuilds would then be fooled into thinking that the main index has more data than it actually does, and the recently added documents would not be indexed by either the main or the delta index. So, our first fix is to replace the `sql_query_post` of the previous example with a `sql_query_post_index` option, which gets run only when indexing was definitely successful.

Second problem: what if insertions were made into the documents table while we were indexing? Those documents would go missing from both the main and delta indexes. They wouldn't be in the main one because SELECT from sql_query never actually saw them (it began executing before they even were inserted), and they wouldn't be in the delta one either because they are erroneously covered by the MAX (id) fetched after the main indexing. So, we need to be consistent about what we actually index and what we track. One way to attain that is to compute MAX (id) once in the beginning using a pre-query, and referring to that value.

The third problem now arises as a new consequence of the two fixes. It's tempting and pretty handy to store MAX (id) into a session variable. But a post-index query runs over a separate connection. So we'll need to temporarily persist that variable into a database; otherwise, sql_query_post_index would never see it.

As a final touch, it helps in terms of maintenance to move common access details into a separate source and inherit from that source rather than copy sql_host and its friends many times.

With all those changes applied, we get something like this:

```
source base
{
    type          = mysql
    sql_host      = localhost
    sql_user      = root
    sql_pass      =
    sql_db        = test
}

source srcmain : base
{
    sql_query_pre  = SET @maxid:=(SELECT MAX(id) FROM documents)
    sql_query      = SELECT * FROM documents WHERE id<=@maxid
    sql_query_post = REPLACE INTO sphinxcounters \
        VALUES ('documents_tmp', @maxid)
    sql_query_post_index = DELETE FROM sphinxcounters \
        WHERE tablename='documents'
    sql_query_post_index = UPDATE sphinxcounters \
        SET tablename='documents' WHERE tablename='documents_tmp'
}
```

That's a bit more clunky, but much more fail-proof now. There's still a window for a type of failure that would require some manual intervention to clean up, but it's so much smaller now.

With the previous setup and database changes preemptively run in sql_query_post, any indexing problem that happens during a rather long stretch of indexing work that follows fetching the rows (say, if *indexer* runs out of disk space, or crashes, or gets accidentally killed, etc.) would leave your instance in an inconsistent state. The helper counters table would incorrectly suggest that the new main index is safely in place when, in fact, it has gone missing. And, until the next main index rebuild, the newly added data that was supposed to be turned in this update would not actually be available for searching.

With the `sql_query_post_index` setup just shown, that inconsistency is no longer possible, as the helper table only gets changes after the index is actually in place. If anything happens before this, the previous state (the last successfully built main index and the respective `maxid` value) is consistent, so the new copy of an index would just get cleanly re-created from scratch. If anything happens after this, the new state would be consistent. (In the worst case, *.new.sp** files would not actually be picked up by *searchd* in a timely manner, but they would automatically be picked up the next time *searchd* starts.) So, pretty much the only way to achieve inconsistency is to crash the database between the two post-index queries, and even in that highly improbable case, you'd only need to manually rerun the second query. (Alternatively, if the helper table is transactional, you could begin the post-index statements with `BEGIN` and end them with `COMMIT` so that the entire batch of changes is atomic, that is, it either applies in full or fails and does not apply at all.)

So far so good; let's conjure a delta source definition next:

```
source srcdelta : base
{
    sql_query       = SELECT * FROM documents WHERE id>(SELECT maxid \
        FROM sphinxcounters WHERE tablename='documents')
}
```

Wow, that was easy. We pull all new documents, defined as those with an ID greater than the maximum indexed one, and that is it.

Except you have to be careful what you inherit. The example just shown is correct, because we inherit everything from a base source, and we only get SQL access from it. However, if `srcdelta` just inherited from `srcmain`, only overriding `sql_query`, that'd be a mistake again—because pre- and post-queries would also inherit, and you'd need to explicitly shut them off.

```
source srcdelta : srcmain
{
    sql_query_pre =
    sql_query       = SELECT * FROM documents WHERE id>(SELECT maxid \
        FROM sphinxcounters WHERE tablename='documents')
    sql_query_post =
    sql_query_post_index =
}
```

This very particular setup case can be simplified a bit, though. Sphinx internally keeps track of the last document ID it indexed and makes it available in the post-index query via a `$maxid` macro variable, relieving us from the need to manually track it via the database (not that our earlier examples were in vain; on the contrary, we'll refer to them a lot in upcoming sections).

```
source srcmain : base
{
```

```
    sql_query       = SELECT * FROM documents
    sql_query_post_index = REPLACE INTO sphinxcounters \
        VALUES ('documents', $maxid)
}
```

That concludes the simplest "append-only database" example. We can now set up the main and delta indexes properly, and rotate the delta index seamlessly without interfering with the searches. On to more complex tasks...

Handling Updates and Deletions with K-Lists

An insert-only strategy for adding new documents real quick covers a number of common tasks, such as archival of never-ever-changing documents (think of sent emails), but other scenarios call for document updates and deletions. RT indexes can do both transparently, but that comes at a price, so "manual" updates and deletions with plain indexes are nevertheless of interest.

In relation to search, there are two very different kinds of updates.

First, you might need to update document attributes but not document content. Sphinx lets you do that instantly with any index type with the UpdateAttributes() API call and the UPDATE statement in SphinxQL. (As a side note, these updates are a bit different from what you would get in a transactional database. They are "slightly atomic," that is, atomic on a column value level only. That means you never get an invalid column value; the only option is either the valid old value or valid new value. But at the same time, an already running query can "see" and be affected by a concurrent update. You can't see half an update on a row, though, because Sphinx currently allows updating one column at a time only.)

Second, you might need to update document text content. In an ideal world, a search engine would be able to update its full-text index on the fly very quickly without sacrificing any robustness or performance. In the real world, those updates have to sacrifice search performance to an extent that reflects the chosen index format. There's always a trade-off between index update speed and search speed. Basically, the better the index format is suited to serve search queries, the worse it is suited for updates, and vice versa. Sphinx's disk index format is optimized for the utmost search and batch indexing performance, and as a consequence, updates of the full-text index itself are practically impossible.

Yet we can still set them up to go into a delta index along with totally new documents, exactly as we just did with those insertions.

Unsophisticated partitioning based on document ID won't work in this scenario, as updates don't necessarily change the ID. Thus, we need a new column that stores the last updated timestamp along with each document. Some data already comes with a suitable column; when data doesn't, it should be easy to add one. For instance, a TIMESTAMP column type in MySQL can be declared with the ON UPDATE CURRENT_TIME

STAMP option, which will automatically update a column whenever the row is changed. And we'll also need to update our helper table to carry timestamps instead of IDs.

```
CREATE TABLE sphinxcounters (
    tablename VARCHAR(255) NOT NULL PRIMARY KEY,
    maxts TIMESTAMP NOT NULL );

ALTER TABLE documents
    ADD COLUMN ts TIMESTAMP NOT NULL ON UPDATE CURRENT_TIMESTAMP;
```

So, just add a TIMESTAMP column, replace references to IDs with references to timestamps in the previous example, and we're all set, right? Oh, and we can also use the current time instead of computing a maximum value off the database:

```
source srcmain : base
{
    sql_query_pre  = SET @maxts:=(SELECT NOW())
    sql_query      = SELECT * FROM documents WHERE ts<=@maxts
    . . .
    # WRONG!
}
```

We're almost there. Except that timestamps in place of IDs introduce a new and shiny catch. IDs, being primary keys, are unique. Timestamps are not. No two rows can share the same ID, but a great many rows can share the same timestamp. Also, timestamps usually come with a resolution of one second, and a lot can happen in a second. So, using WHERE ts<=@maxts to pick rows for the main index and WHERE ts>@maxts for the delta index, respectively (by a blind analogy with IDs), is prone to missing rows, ones that were inserted during the *remainder* of that second when sql_query began.

Indeed, imagine that we memorize @maxts at 06:00:00.300, that is, 0.3 seconds past 6:00 a.m. sharp. The timestamp we get is trimmed to a whole second, ending up as 06:00:00. And queries are quick, so we're still within that second—say, at 06:00:00.350, when we begin to fetch rows with ts<=@maxts into the main index. Then at 06:00:00.500, a new row gets inserted by a concurrent client. It fits the ts<=@maxts condition, but our sql_query already executes and won't see it. And a subsequent delta index rebuild would refuse this row too, because it does not fit the ts>@maxts condition. So, it gets lost.

Using WHERE ts>=@maxts for the delta index is a solution, but not a very good one, as that way we'll duplicate some of the rows with ts=@maxts in both the main and delta indexes.

The proper solution is to use WHERE ts<@maxts as a condition for the main index, and WHERE ts>=@maxts for the delta one. That way, rows added during the very last fraction of a second before the indexing takes place don't make it into the main index, but they get included into the delta index the next time it is built. No rows are lost, and no rows are duplicated.

```
source srcmain : base
{
```

```
    sql_query_pre  = SET @maxts:=(SELECT NOW())
    sql_query      = SELECT * FROM documents WHERE ts<@maxts
    . . .
}

source srcdelta : base
{
    sql_query      = SELECT * FROM documents WHERE ts>=(SELECT maxts \
        FROM sphinxcounters WHERE tablename='documents')
}
```

One more subtle catch successfully resolved by The Hardy Boys! Time is continuous, whereas timestamps correspond to spans of time, so pay attention and be careful, says Frank.

I see dead keywords, says Joe.

Wait, what?!

Searching for a keyword present in a new document version that resides in the delta index is guaranteed to return expected results in any case. Even if that keyword matches the old version of a document that exists in the main index, and both matches make it into internal per-index result sets, the new match "shadows" the old match. When the indexes are queried in the right order, that is:

```
// API way
$client->Query ( "keyword", "idxmain, idxdelta" );

// SphinxQL way
SELECT * FROM idxmain, idxdelta WHERE MATCH('keyword');
```

However, if we search for an *old* keyword that only exists in the main index, we get only that single match. We don't get any matches from the delta index and nothing shadows the older, now-wrong match. That's a so-called *phantom* match. The old document version is no longer part of the actual users' collection and should no longer be retrieved, as there's a new superseding version now. But we can still retrieve a phantom of the old document by querying for an old keyword.

Another related case is when a keyword matches both the main and delta indexes, but the latter match does not make it into an internal delta's result set. We get an old match that we should not have gotten.

Deletions pose the same problem. The delta index does not have any document to shadow the supposedly deleted one, so old rows will keep being returned on matched keywords.

The root cause of all three manifestations is the very same: namely, Sphinx does not know that document number 123 in index idxmain is now deprecated in favor of a newer version in index idxdelta, or just deleted. We need to tell it to ignore the obsolete parts of the index. Well, if there's a will, there's a way. (And, eerily Perl-ishly, there's even more than one way to do it.)

For the sake of completeness, one way to get Sphinx in the know is to create a separate document attribute that tells whether the Sphinx-side document is alive, and to update it on the fly when the database-side row gets updated or deleted. Then filter on that attribute when searching. That's rather fragile, tricky to implement, prone to various errors, and generally discouraged.

A better way is to use a *kill-list* (or, more simply, a *K-list*). This is a list of document IDs attached to an index XYZ that specifies what documents should be suppressed from search results in any other indexes that precede XYZ in a query index list. The K-list never affects the index it's attached to.

In main+delta scheme terms, a K-list attached to the *delta* index is a list of IDs that need to be thrown away from the *main* index. Attaching a K-list to the main one is pointless, as no indexes would ever precede it in the query, and its K-list would never affect anything. Having the K-list for the main index stored in the delta one also means we never have to touch the main one at all after we build it. Rather, we maintain a list of no longer needed rows from the main index and plug it into the delta index as our K-list.

A K-list can (and should) be used both to fight phantoms and to implement deletions. "Kill" all recently changed documents in our delta index, and phantoms are no longer. Add a list of recently deleted documents, and deletions are nicely handled too. "Recently" would be defined as "since the last successful rebuild of the main index" here. The list of changed documents is trivial to extract with the aid of a timestamp field, but a list of deleted rows (perhaps with a deletion timestamp) should be additionally maintained. Either a minor change in the application or a trigger in the database should normally suffice.

```
mysql> CREATE TABLE sphinxklist (
    -> id INTEGER NOT NULL,
    -> ts TIMESTAMP NOT NULL );
Query OK, 0 rows affected (0.25 sec)

mysql> DELIMITER //
mysql> CREATE TRIGGER sphinxklist
    -> AFTER DELETE ON documents
    -> FOR EACH ROW BEGIN
    ->     INSERT INTO sphinxklist VALUES (OLD.id, NOW());
    -> END
    -> //
Query OK, 0 rows affected (0.00 sec)
```

Another small change fishes out both updated IDs from the documents table and killed IDs from the helper sphinxklist table we just created, and puts them into the delta index:

```
source srcdelta : base
{
    sql_query_pre       = SET @maxts:= (SELECT maxts \
        FROM sphinxcounters WHERE tablename='documents')
    sql_query           = SELECT * FROM documents WHERE ts>=@maxts
```

```
    sql_query_killlist = SELECT id FROM documents WHERE ts>=@maxts \
        UNION SELECT id FROM sphinxklist
}
```

Now for a finishing touch: one more post-index query to properly clean up old rows from the sphinxklist helper once we rebuild the main index.

```
source srcmain : base
{
    . . .
    sql_query_post_index = DELETE FROM sphinxklist \
        WHERE ts<(SELECT maxts FROM sphinxcounters \
            WHERE tablename='documents')
}
```

And we're all set! Data changes that get reflected in Sphinx search results very quickly through reindexing a tiny delta index? Check. Inserts, deletes, updates? Check. No more phantoms? Check. Hooray!

Dead keywords are still plaguing us, because the K-list cannot affect keyword statistics, and if a keyword matches 1,000 documents in the main index, it will report 1,000 matches even if 900 of them are now killed. But all the wilder things (spooky phantoms) are now gone.

Assembled from bits and changes back to its full glory, the latest version of an example configuration that picks documents based on timestamps and handles everything now looks as follows:

```
source srcmain : base
{
    sql_query_pre        = SET @maxts:=(SELECT NOW())
    sql_query            = SELECT * FROM documents WHERE ts<@maxts
    sql_query_post       = REPLACE INTO sphinxcounters \
        VALUES ('documents_tmp', @maxts)
    sql_query_post_index = DELETE FROM sphinxcounters \
        WHERE tablename='documents'
    sql_query_post_index = UPDATE sphinxcounters \
        SET tablename='documents' WHERE tablename='documents_tmp'
    sql_query_post_index = DELETE FROM sphinxklist \
        WHERE ts<(SELECT maxts FROM sphinxcounters \
            WHERE tablename='documents')
}

source srcdelta : base
{
    sql_query_pre        = SET @maxts:= (SELECT maxts \
        FROM sphinxcounters WHERE tablename='documents')
    sql_query            = SELECT * FROM documents WHERE ts>=@maxts
    sql_query_killlist   = SELECT id FROM documents WHERE ts>=@maxts \
        UNION SELECT id FROM sphinxklist
}
```

With functionality (as in handling inserts, updates, and deletes) fully covered, it's time we fiddled about performance again.

Scheduling Rebuilds, and Using Multiple Deltas

Our hardened main+delta setup can deal with all kinds of data changes now, but we still need to discuss exactly how to schedule regular delta index rebuilds. In addition, there is a question of what happens tomorrow, or in a week, when more and more data flows in, and the delta naturally grows.

Let's go back to the sizing numbers we chose before: 10 MB/second text indexing speed, 10 million documents in the archive collection, 10,000 documents added daily, and 20 KB per average document. Since we're also handling updates now, let's make that 10,000 added and 10,000 updated documents, totaling 20,000 documents, or 400 MB of data.

So, our daily data set takes 40 seconds to reindex by the end of the day. Tomorrow, that figure doubles, to 80 seconds. By the end of the week it's 200 seconds. In a year, 10,000 seconds or almost three hours, and we're sort of back to square one. Not cool.

Deltas grow over time, so we need to occasionally rebuild our main index just as well. When do we do it? And while we're at it, when do we rebuild the deltas?

That gets determined by your requirements. Suppose it's OK for the documents to become visible in the search results within an hour. You can schedule delta index rebuilds to happen every hour, and then schedule main index rebuilds in such a way that the delta index can never grow so large that it takes more than an hour to build. For instance, we can rebuild our fictional 10 million-strong main index once every four weeks on Saturday night. Then even the worst-case delta rebuild (which is the one taking place a bit earlier that very Saturday evening) would not take more than 800 seconds, according to our estimates. Estimates can be wrong all the time, especially in the IT business and in construction, but we just need the rebuild to take place in fewer than 3,600 seconds, so there's plenty of headroom.

Come to think of it, Saturday night is probably the low point each week, so we can easily go faster. Schedule weekly instead of monthly main index rebuilds, and the delta index should take less than 200 seconds to rebuild. That allows us to schedule delta rebuilds every five minutes.

OK, but can we go faster than five minutes while continuing to perform costly main rebuilds weekly?

Yes. We discussed only a setup with a single main and delta index so far. But nothing prevents us from having two or more deltas. And Sphinx can cope with searching through three indexes just as well as through two. (Or 100, actually, although 100 would bring in a few extra implications.)

So, let's now set up *two* deltas: one that covers everything since the last (weekly) main index rebuild until today, and another one that covers just today. The first delta would need to be rebuilt on a daily basis, and take less than 200 seconds per day. The second one would carry, at most, 20,000 documents and take less than 40 seconds. The second one can be run as frequently as every minute.

Rebuilds that happen every minute, or less often, are interesting on a number of levels. First, they map to standard Unix cron jobs (or Windows scheduled tasks) easily. So, you can schedule all your indexers using trusty, good old crontab. Second, updates will take, at most, 60 seconds, and 30 seconds on average. That's quick enough for a great many applications. Even such a seemingly dynamic application as an online auction website would barely need to update *text* content quicker than that (as I mentioned attribute updates are instantaneous and could contain time-sensitive bid information). Third, only so much data can usually be procured in a minute, making the respective deltas rather small and amenable to frequent indexing.

Returning to our recurring example, if our 20,000-document updates are distributed more or less evenly over eight work hours, this makes an average of 40 updates per minute. Updates would never be distributed *that* evenly, of course, but even if we plan for 50 times the peak value, that's 2,000 updates, or 40 MB of data, or just four seconds to spend indexing every minute. This is clearly feasible.

So, when brute delta force does not work, you are just not using enough deltas. (Yes, I am exaggerating to make a point.)

How many deltas should be deployed? The exact figure depends on your requirements, spare server power that can be spent on reindexing, and all that jazz, but generally only a few will suffice. Each delta layer should index many times less data than the previous one, and an exponential function grows extremely fast. After all, in our example we can reach an indexing lag against a *200 GB collection* measured in *seconds* with just three deltas—week-to-date, day-to-hour, and last-hour.

Deltas can go in the other direction too, to further reduce the amount of rebuild work, but there's more to that than just deltas.

Merge Versus Rebuild Versus Deltas

The Sphinx batch indexer can create indexes not only by plucking data out of the database, but also by *merging* two existing indexes together.

```
$ indexer --merge dstindex srcindex
```

Basically, the preceding command means "merge data from `srcindex` into `dstindex`". Only `dstindex` files get written to during the merge; `srcindex` files stay read-only. Usually, `dstindex` would be a main index, and `srcindex` a delta index in a main+delta setup scheme.

Merging doesn't touch the database (more accurately, data sources) at all. That results in both an upside and a downside. The upside is that the database server doesn't get any extra load, and that the process completes faster overall than indexing. The downside is that the *indexer* run doesn't pull the latest updates from the database, and that extra steps have to be "manually" taken to update the helper counter tables or perform any other required post-merge maintenance on the database side.

Merging supports the `--rotate` option and plays nicely with rotation, does index locking and creates a shadow copy as needed, and on the whole works with index files precisely as regular indexing does.

```
$ indexer --merge idxmain idxdelta --rotate
```

The preceding code merges everything in the `idxdelta` index into the `idxmain` index, creating a new version of the latter (in *.new.sp** files), and then sends SIGHUP to *searchd* so that it will pick up the new version.

The output index receives all rows from `idxmain` except (a) those that are explicitly killed in a K-list attached to `idxdelta`, and (b) those that can also be found in `idxdelta`. It also receives all rows from `idxdelta`, without any constraints. As a consequence of (b), there will automatically be no phantoms for updated rows after the merge, even when the delta index has no K-list. Also, keyword statistics get updated. The overall result is that searches against the merged index are expected to deliver exactly the same results that searches against both indexes did—except that the merged index can be even more correct because it has updated keyword statistics and excludes phantoms.

Since no database work happens during the index merge, all data has to come from the index files on disk. It's important to understand that merging does *not* super-quickly embed the delta index data into the main files using only a few wisps of work and a whiff of pixie dust. It does *create* a new version of the main index, and for that, it has to read the *entire* contents of both the main and delta source indexes, and write the entire contents of the new index. So, if you're merging a 100 GB index against a 1 GB one, expect approximately 202 GB worth of disk I/O, half reads and half writes.

Often that's still faster than extricating 100 GB from a database and doing 200 GB of disk writes, as you'd need with regular, nondelta indexing.

A small experiment I ran can give you a sense of what real numbers could look like. With everything fully cached in RAM (including the data in the database as well as both small indexes involved), merging a 10,000-document, 8.1 MB index into a 100,000-document, 73.6 MB index took 2.96 seconds, with 1.06 seconds spent writing the resultant files. Directly indexing the 110,000-document collection took 13.01 seconds, with 1.70 seconds spent doing writes. The resultant indexes were byte-wise identical. In the end, they contained the very same data, though obtained in two different ways.

The improvement of merging: three seconds total merging instead of 13 seconds total indexing, a 4x improvement, plus no database impact. And fewer disk writes. Could be worth considering.

Reindexing the main index comes with an extra perk, though, of running all those pre-, post-, and post-index queries we took such pains to define in our configuration earlier. With merge, one has to jump through a few hoops to do the needed changes in helper tables. Namely, check the *indexer* return code for success (which is zero), and run the

SQL queries that ought to be run—juggle the threshold timestamps, mop up the K-list table, and do other tidying up. In our fine example a few sections afore, we'd now need to compute and store the maxts value for the delta index too, and promote it as maxts for the main index when the merge succeeds, then call *indexer* again to build a fresh, (almost) empty delta index.

```
source srcdelta : base
{
    sql_query_pre       = SET @maxts:= (SELECT maxts \
        FROM sphinxcounters WHERE tablename='documents')
    sql_query_pre       = SET @maxtsdelta:= (SELECT NOW())
    sql_query           = SELECT * FROM documents WHERE ts>=@maxts \
        AND ts<@maxtsdelta
    sql_query_killlist  = SELECT id FROM documents WHERE ts>=@maxts \
        AND ts<@maxtsdelta UNION SELECT id FROM sphinxklist
    sql_query_post      = REPLACE INTO sphinxcounters \
        VALUES ('documents_delta_tmp', @maxtsdelta)
    sql_query_post_index = DELETE FROM sphinxcounters \
        WHERE tablename='documents_delta_tmp'
    sql_query_post_index = UPDATE sphinxcounters \
        SET tablename='documents_delta' \
        WHERE tablename='documents_delta_tmp'
}
```

We need just a few more lines to complement these delta index setup changes. One is an SQL script to run when the merge is successful:

```
SET @maxts:=(SELECT maxts FROM sphinxcounters
    WHERE tablename='documents_delta');
UPDATE sphinxcounters SET maxts=@maxts
    WHERE tablename='documents';
```

Next, a shell script to check how merging went, fire that SQL script, and rebuild the delta index too:

```
#!/bin/sh
indexer --rotate --merge idxmain idxdelta
if [ "$?" -eq "0" ]; then
    cat post_merge.sql | mysql -u root test
    indexer --rotate idxdelta
fi
```

That's pretty much it, more or less the complete kickoff guide to counters-related trickery versus index merge.

Last but not least, the --merge-klists option is useful for merging delta indexes, in case you have more than one and need to merge them.

The default merge behavior is to apply and copy the K-list from srcindex to dstindex (a.k.a. the delta and main indexes in the most frequent case). The K-list attached to dstindex, if any, is discarded.

When --merge-klists is specified, the srcindex K-list is not used, and the dstindex K-list is not discarded. Instead, they get merged together and the derived common K-list is attached to the resultant new version of dstindex. This is useful for merging two delta indexes.

Scripting and Reloading Configurations

Two last bits left standing for this chapter are a discussion of inserting dynamic scripts into the *sphinx.conf* configuration file, and how *searchd* reloads the configuration file on the fly and adjusts the set of served indexes accordingly.

Scripting automatically engages when you use shell-like shebang syntax in the very first *sphinx.conf* line. Both *indexer* and *searchd* detect that, invoke the specified interpreter, and parse its output.

```
#!/usr/bin/php
<?php for ($i=1; $i<=4; $i++) { ?>
source chunk<?=$i?>
{
    sql_host = localhost
    sql_user = root
    sql_pass =
    sql_db   = dbchunk<?=$i?>
    . . .
}
<?php } // end source loop ?>
```

You can use any scripting language you prefer, as long as the script output is a valid *sphinx.conf* configuration.

Scripted or not, the configuration file is reloaded by *searchd* and scanned for changes on SIGHUP, causing the daemon to change configured indexes. (The reloading also changes the index data that rotation brings in.)

So you can, for instance, add a new index to *sphinx.conf*, have *indexer* build it (without having to use --rotate since it's not yet loaded by *searchd*), and then send SIGHUP to *searchd* and begin querying in your application. The same holds true for removals. Indexes removed from the configuration file will stop being serviced by *searchd* once it reloads the configuration.

Note that index-level settings that affect indexing-time text processing (such as the character set type and valid characters table, HTML stripping, morphology, etc.) are embedded into the index data and will *not* get reloaded and applied. They require an index rebuild to take effect and the rebuilt index needs to be rotated into *searchd*.

However, there also are a few index-level settings that can be changed in the runtime and reside in the configuration file only: mlock, enable_star, and expand_keywords. Those will take effect immediately upon a SIGHUP.

CHAPTER 6

Relevance and Ranking

You're now armed with a good chunk of knowledge about getting up and running with Sphinx, creating and managing indexes, and writing proper queries. However, there's one more skill that's of use with nearly every site: improving search quality. So, let's spend some time discussing quality in general and what Sphinx can offer, shall we?

Relevance Assessment: A Black Art

We can't really chase down "search quality" until we formally define it and decide how we measure it. An empirical approach, as in "Here, I just made up another custom ranking rule out of thin air and I think it will generally improve our results any time of day," wears out very soon. After about the third such rule, you can no longer manage such an approach, because the total number of rule combinations explodes combinatorially, and arguing about (not to mention proving) the value of every single combination quickly becomes impossible. A scientific approach, as in "Let us introduce some comprehensible numerical metrics that can be computed programmatically and then grasped intuitively," yields to automation and scales somewhat better.

So, what *is* search quality? Chapter 1 mentioned that documents in the result set are, by default, ordered using a *relevance ranking* function that assigns a different weight to every document, based on the current query, document contents, other document attributes, and other factors. But it's very important to realize that the relevance value that is computed by a search engine means little with regard to the relevancy of the document in the eyes of the human beholder. A document that an engine ranks very high can still very well be junk. (Do you want proof? You've never seen any spam in Google search results? I so envy you.) And vice versa: one document that you need might get ranked low.

So, simply matching keywords to documents does not have much to do with quality. When the *relevant* documents that you were really looking for are among the first, top-rated results, quality is high. But when the top *N* results are polluted with spam, junk, or *irrelevant* documents that honestly match requested keywords but aren't the ones you were looking for, quality is low.

Getting to true relevance—from a human point of view—is harder than defining filters and word rankings. Although saying so may initially seem controversial, "human" relevance can't actually be automated. Not at all, ever. Given a document and a query, there's no way for a machine to tell whether the document is relevant to a query from a human point of view—let alone to compute "how" relevant the document is. Any matching document could be a spam page that has all the keywords, or even legitimate, informative content that simply does not really answer the query. Moreover, different people might treat the same document differently. So, relevance is not just impossible to automate. Relevance is subjective.

Despite this semantic principle, we still need to rank our results somehow. And we still need to be able to compare different "machine" relevance ranking algorithms. So, if we can't have the machine answer "relevant or not" questions, we need to use human *assessors*. And because their *judgments* about the relevance are subjective, ideally we also want every document/query pair to be assessed by several different assessors. That sounds like a daunting task, and it is. But this is indeed how quality improvement works in reality, and so far the only known way it probably could work. Human assessors are given a query and a set of documents, and are asked to say whether each document is relevant or not. Sometimes they render nonbinary opinions: for instance, whether the document is "barely" relevant or "very" relevant, or even assign a relevance score from A to F.

Once we know which documents are relevant, we can introduce a number of statistical *quality metrics*. Note that quality metrics aren't something that a search engine computes—they are something used to characterize search engines. On a large scale, they can serve the purpose of comparing the quality of search results between two search engines. They can also be used to rate the quality of two different ranking functions provided by the same search engine.

It's worth noting that there's no single rule-them-all quality metric, either. Different scenarios can call for different metrics. Web engines strive to make sure that a lot of relevant documents are among the top 10, because most users never go past page 1, so the metric one would want to optimize above all would be NDCG@10 or an equivalent (don't worry, I'll explain what NDCG and other metrics are shortly). On the other hand, the user of a search engine for legal filings can be expected to be noticeably more persistent about the amount of documents she has to rummage through, and very concerned not to miss even a single relevant one. In that case, end-user satisfaction would be better modeled with an R@1000 metric instead of an NDCG@10 one. As they would probably say in London, "Needs must when the lawyer searches."

Two classic (even ancient) metrics are precision and recall. *Precision* is defined as the ratio between the number of relevant documents returned and the total number of documents returned. *Recall* is defined as the ratio of the number of relevant documents returned to the total number of relevant documents existing in our collection. Represented as formulas, the metrics are:

$$Precision = \frac{RelevantDocumentsFound}{TotalDocumentsFound}$$

$$Recall = \frac{RelevantDocumentsFound}{TotalRelevantDocuments}$$

So, precision tells us how good our result set is, and maxes out at 1.0 when all the found documents are relevant. Recall indicates how complete the result set is, and maxes out at 1.0 when all relevant documents are retrieved.

However, precision and recall measure the results as a set, and don't take ordering into account. Therefore, they do not show any difference between an algorithm that puts all relevant results first and an algorithm that puts them last, and can't really be used to compare two such relevance ranking algorithms. Fortunately, there are other, more practical metrics, built on the same idea.

Precision-at-N, abbreviated as *P@N*, is the ratio of relevant documents within the first N results returned. For example, a P@10 value of 0.7 means that 7 of 10 of the first documents were relevant.

$$P@N = \frac{RelevantDocumentsWithinFirstN}{N}$$

The preceding formula assumes that every document is either relevant or irrelevant, a binary quality. Another way to calculate P@N is to define *score(i)* along a range from 0 to 1, where 0 means the document returned at position number *i* is judged to be totally irrelevant, and 1 means it's extremely relevant. Then calculate:

$$P@N = \sum_{i=1}^{N} \frac{score(i)}{N}$$

This method still does not take the ordering within those top N documents into account, which is a serious lapse when one reads that many people tend to stick to the top three results returned by search engines. So, P@N is further extended to a metric called *average precision* (AP), which computes P@N for every N that represents the position of a relevant document in our result, and then averages the values.

For instance, suppose the first and tenth documents are relevant, and all others are not. We calculate P@1, which is 1.0 (one out of one top document is relevant), and P@10, which is 0.2 (2 out of 10 documents are relevant). The AP@10 is (1.0+0.2)/2=0.6. In terms of a formula, AP@N is:

$$MAP@N = \frac{\sum_{i=1}^{N} score(i)\,P@i}{\sum_{i=1}^{N} score(i)}$$

This definition uses the same generalized, floating-point *score(i)* and thus also works in cases when relevance judgments aren't binary. When they are binary, average precision reduces to a rather simple effect: it is the average of all precision values taken at every position in which there is a relevant document, averaged over all the relevant documents in the top *N* result set.

Another popular metric is *discounted cumulative gain* (DCG), defined as the sum of assessor-assigned scores divided by a logarithmic falloff factor. Basically, a highly relevant document scores 1.0 if it comes up first in the results, but only 0.5 if it comes up third. The formula is:

$$DCG@N = \sum_{i=1...n} \frac{score(i)}{\log_2(1+i)}$$

DCG also allows for nonbinary relevance judgments, given, for instance, on a score of 0 to 2 where 0 is irrelevant, 1 is relevant, and 2 is highly relevant.

In addition to AP and DCG, several other result set metrics fold multiple per-document relevance judgments into a single value: normalized DCG (NDCG), Bpref, mean reciprocal rank (MRR), graded MRR (GMRR), pFound, and more.

All the metrics mentioned so far deal with single queries, and to determine how well search engines perform, one needs to evaluate sets of many queries. That's done by simply averaging the metric value of all the queries. In the search literature, averaged AP is called MAP, or mean average precision. Other metrics are usually referred to by their original name, because it's clear from the context whether we're talking about a single query or an average result achieved over all queries.

As you can see, the math behind quality assessment is pretty simple. But whatever quality metric we use, its core is always that *score(i)* term, and that has to be evaluated by a human being—or, better, by a platoon of them. The more assessors one can use and the more queries you can feed them, the better overall assessment quality you'll get. But the judgments will always be subjective anyway, and assessment results will always be tied to the particular queries used and the document sets retrieved.

Relevance Ranking Functions

To refresh your memory, relevance ranking functions take a number of different factors into account and compute a single relevance value for every given document.

Possible factors abound. Major web search engines, striving for top-notch, state-of-the-art ranking quality, account for *hundreds* of different ranking factors.

So-called *text factors* depend on the document, the query, or the entire document collection text. Typical factors include:

- How many times did our keywords occur within the matched document?
- How many times were they repeated in the query?
- How frequently does every keyword occur in the entire document collection?
- Do the keywords occur in the document in exactly the same order as they occur in the query? If not, are they at least close to each other, or are they scattered all around the document?
- Where do they occur: in the title field, or in the main content field, near the beginning, or near the end?
- Did we match the query keyword form exactly, or is it a stemmed match?
- In how big a font was a keyword written on the HTML page?

Answers to questions such as these provide text-based factors that a search engine can use to compute its magic relevance value.

Nontext factors are important as well. On a forum site, you might want to boost posts made by moderators in the search results. Or users with lots of hard-earned karma. Or threads that were unusually trafficked. Or, as is usually the case in production, all of the above. On a news site search, an important nontext factor is how recent the found document is. One well-known web search factor is PageRank, which is also a nontext factor. The text in a hyperlink (URL) could arguably be either a text factor or a nontext factor.

Ranking factors are different from sorting conditions, even though in the end they serve the same purpose (ordering the search results), and might use the very same data. Factors affect weights, and therefore the ordering of the results, but in a not-so-obvious way, whereas sorting conditions are used strictly for ordering.

To understand the distinction I'm making, consider a search on a news site. Assume that we can compute a text-based weight ranging from 0.0 to 1.0, and that we also have a publication date. When we boost our text weight by 0.1 for last-day articles, 0.05 for last-week articles, and 0.02 for last-month articles, it's a weighting factor. However, it's just one of the factors, and highly relevant matches posted a year ago will be able to outweigh barely relevant ones posted minutes ago. But we can also use the very same date as our primary sorting condition so that results from yesterday are guaranteed to come before results from last year, no matter what their text-based relevance rank (weight) is. We're using the very same data, maybe even in the very same manner (sorting with that date-based 0.1/0.05/0.02 boost), but now it's a sorting condition, and not a weighting factor.

One famous text-based ranking function is called *Okapi BM25* (or *BM25* for brevity). It was developed back in the early 1980s, but is still in wide use. The key idea of BM25 is to rank documents higher if they have rare keywords and if they have many occurrences of a keyword. The BM25 weight is computed as:

$$BM25 = \sum_{i=1}^{W} \frac{TF(i)(1+k)}{TF(i)+k\left(1-b+b\dfrac{DL}{avgDL}\right)} IDF(i)$$

$$IDF(i) = \frac{\log\left(\dfrac{N-n+1}{n}\right)}{\log(N)}$$

where:

- *W* is the number of keywords.
- *TF(i)* is *term frequency*, that is, the number of times the ith keyword occurred in the document being ranked.
- *IDF(i)* is *inverse document frequency*, that is, a normalized frequency of the ith keyword in our entire document collection.
- *N* is the number of documents in our entire collection.
- *n* is the number of documents that match the ith keyword.
- *DL* is the current document length.
- *avgDL* is the average document length in our collection.
- *k* and *b* are magic constants (e.g., *k* = 1.2, *b* = 0.75).

The *IDF(i)* factor is the part that assigns more weight to rare keywords. It ranges from -1.0 when *n* = *N* (i.e., the keyword occurs in all documents) to 1.0 when *n* = 1 (the keyword occurs in exactly one document), and reaches 0.0 when *n* = (*N*+1)/2. So, it's best when the keyword is so rare that it only occurs in a single document, and it's worst when the keyword occurs in every document. Note that when the keyword occurs in more than half of the documents indexed, IDF gets negative, and matching the keyword actually hurts the rank.

This is controversial at first glance, but if there are more documents with the keyword than without it, we are probably more interested in fewer common documents that do not mention an overly frequent keyword. As a crude example, in an aeronautics database, you can expect "airplane" to be mentioned frequently, and the presence of that word does not help determine which documents are of interest to the person conducting the search.

The *TF(i)* part essentially boosts the weight when the keyword occurs several times, and the complex fraction just serves to limit that boost. We could simply multiply *TF(i)* by *IDF(i)*, but in that case a document mentioning one keyword 1,000 times would be ranked way too high. On the other hand, this fraction (simplified under an assumption that our document is of average length or *DL = avgDL*):

$$ClampedTF(i) = \frac{TF(i)(1+k)}{TF(i)+k}$$

is guaranteed to range from 1.0 to 1.0+*k*, growing as *TF(i)* grows but never going over a certain limit. So, *k* is essentially a limit on the boost given to a weight by a term's (a keyword's) frequency within a document.

Finally, the *b* constant controls some length magic that boosts shorter documents. *b* should take a value from 0 to 1. When *b* = 0, document length will not be accounted for at all. When *b* = 1, document length has the greatest possible influence on the BM25 function.

BM25 is important because it's known to work pretty well, and is used in every single search system which does ranking at all. It's a well-known, de facto standard ranking function that is both a good foundation and a good reference—that is, a solid foundation to build more complicated state-of-the-art ranking functions, and a widespread baseline reference model at the same time. Most existing open source systems implement only BM25, in fact.

BM25's major drawback is that it considers only keyword statistics, but does not care how the keywords are located in the document in respect to one another and the query. For instance, it will rank a document that simply mentions all the keywords in diverse places exactly as high as a document that matches the query as a phrase perfectly. For instance, given the query "to be or not to be," BM25 would not boost *Hamlet* above all the documents that contain those common English words (and of course, the words are too common to perform well in BM25 anyway). Usually one would expect verbatim quotes to be ranked higher.

That quality drawback in BM25 was, in fact, one of the reasons I created Sphinx in the first place. Sphinx can do classic BM25 ranking, but it defaults to a combined ranking function that uses BM25 as a secondary factor, and the degree of query phrase versus document match as a primary factor. We call that *phrase proximity ranking*. Hence, with the default Sphinx ranking function, documents with verbatim quotes are guaranteed to be ranked above others, and even documents with partial query subphrase matches are guaranteed to be ranked higher. I will explain Sphinx ranking in more detail in the next section.

Sphinx Rankers Explained

Over time, we added quite a bunch of matching and ranking modes to Sphinx, and we will be adding more. A number of different questions that regularly pop up, ranging from "How do I force this document ranked first?" to "How do I draw one to five stars depending on match quality?", boil down to matching and ranking internals. So let's cover that: just how do the ranking modes work, what weighting factors contribute to the final weight and how, how does one tweak stuff, and so on. And, of course, the stars, our destination.

An extra word of warning first, though: remember and beware that the rankers only work in EXTENDED matching mode. Legacy matching modes discussed in Chapter 4 bind the ranking mode in a strict manner, and thus prevent the SetRanking Mode() API call from working; forgetting that is a common error.

Ranking modes (also called *rankers*) can be formally defined as functions that compute a relevance value (weight) for a given query and document arguments. Whether rankers are implicitly set by choosing a legacy matching mode or explicitly set with the API call or SphinxQL OPTION, the rankers control exactly one thing: the document weight. So, for instance, the following two queries will result in exactly the same weight (and exactly the same processing time), because the MATCH_ALL mode uses proximity ranking:

```
// 1st route
$cl->SetMatchMode ( SPH_MATCH_ALL );
$cl->Query ( "hello world" );

// 2nd route
$cl->SetMatchMode ( SPH_MATCH_EXTENDED2 );
$cl->SetRankingMode (  SPH_RANK_PROXIMITY );
$cl->Query ( "hello world" );
```

Relevance is ultimately subjective, so there's no single one-size-fits-all ranker, and there never will be. One can use many different factors to compute a final weight and myriad ways to combine those factors into a weight. Discussing practical approaches to that is a subject for a separate body of Ph.D. dissertation-grade texts.

The two most important weighting factors that Sphinx computes and uses, as of version 1.10-beta, are the classic statistical BM25 factor, used by most, if not all, search engines since the 1980s, and the Sphinx-specific phrase proximity factor.

BM25 Factor

BM25 is a floating-point value that depends on frequencies of the matched keywords only. Frequencies in question are in-document and in-collection frequencies. Basically, keywords that are rarer and/or occur many times in the document yield more weight to that document.

Standard BM25 implementation is nicely covered in the Wikipedia article on BM25,[*] but Sphinx uses a slightly modified variant. First, for performance reasons, we account

---

for all the keyword occurrences in the document, and not just the matched ones. For instance, an **@title "hello world"** query that only matches a single instance of "hello world" in the title will result in the same BM25 as a **hello world** query that matches all the instances of both keywords everywhere in the document. Any keyword occurrences anywhere in the document, including those not actually matched (perhaps not even in the fields that we limited our search query to), contribute to our version of BM25.

Second, we don't enforce any document attributes, and therefore don't necessarily have a document length, so we ignore document length (equivalent to plugging $b = 0$ into the original BM25). Both changes were intentional, as in our testing, the original BM25 did not result in enough ranking improvement to justify the associated performance impact. The exact BM25 computation that Sphinx uses is, in pseudocode, as follows:

```
BM25 = 0
foreach ( keyword in matching_keywords )
{
    n = total_matching_documents ( keyword )
    N = total_documents_in_collection
    k1 = 1.2

    TF = current_document_occurrence_count ( keyword )
    IDF = log((N-n+1)/n) / log(1+N)
    BM25 = BM25 + TF*IDF/(TF+k1)
}

// normalize to 0..1 range
BM25 = 0.5 + BM25 / ( 2*num_keywords ( query ) )
```

TF means Term Frequency in a document being ranked. It's based on a number of occurrences within a document but smoothed with a hyperbola function so that 1,000 occurrences don't result in a 1,000x improvement over just 1. TF can generally vary from 0 to 1 but, with a chosen $k = 1.2$, it actually varies from 0.4545... to 1.

IDF means Inverse Document Frequency in the entire document set. IDF possesses lesser values for frequent words (such as "the" or "to," etc.) and greater values for rare ones, with peak values being $IDF = 1$ when a keyword occurs in exactly one document, and $IDF = -1$ when it occurs in every indexed document.

So, as you can see from the code a few paragraphs up, BM25 increases when the keywords are rare in the document set and occur many times in a specific document and decreases when the keywords are frequent. It should be noted that overly frequent keywords that match more than half of the indexed documents actually decrease BM25! Indeed, when a keyword occurs in 90 percent of the documents, the documents without it are rarer gems, probably more interesting as such, and deserve more weight.

---

* *http://en.wikipedia.org/wiki/Okapi_BM25*

Phrase Proximity Factor

Phrase proximity factor, unlike BM25, does not care about the keyword frequencies at all, but accounts for the mutual disposition of query keywords in the document. Instead of the keyword frequencies used for BM25, Sphinx analyzes keyword positions in every field and computes phrase proximity value as the longest common subsequence (LCS) length between the query and the document. Basically, per-field phrase proximity is the number of keywords that occurred in the document in exactly the same order as they did in the query. Here are a few examples:

```
query = one two three, field = one and two three
field_phrase_weight = 2 (because 2-keyword long "two three" subphrase matched)

query = one two three, field = one and two and three
field_phrase_weight = 1 (because single keywords matched but no subphrase did)

query = one two three, field = nothing matches at all
field_phrase_weight = 0
```

Per-field phrase weights are then multiplied by the per-field user weights specified in a SetFieldWeights() API call (or OPTION field_weights in SphinxQL) and are added together to produce a per-document phrase weight. Field weights default to 1, and can't be set lower than 1. In pseudocode, the entire phrase proximity calculation looks as follows:

```
doc_phrase_weight = 0
foreach ( field in matching_fields )
{
    field_phrase_weight = max_common_subsequence_length ( query, field )
    doc_phrase_weight += user_weight ( field ) * field_phrase_weight
}
```

Here is an example:

```
query = hello world
doc_title = hello world
doc_body = the world is a wonderful place

query_title_weight = 5
query_body_weight = 3

title_phrase_weight = 2
body_phrase_weight = 1
doc_phrase_weight = 2*5+3*1 = 13
```

It's the phrase proximity factor that guarantees that closer phrase matches will be ranked higher, and exact phrase matches will be ranked at the very top. One can use field weights to tweak and tune that behavior. For instance, in the example just shown, a single-keyword match in the title is made to be worth the same as a two-keyword phrase match in the body.

Phrase proximity is, by design, somewhat more computationally intensive than BM25 because it needs to work through all the keyword occurrences in the matched documents and not just the documents only. Sphinx defaults to using proximity because we believe this yields better search quality. You can, however, choose to use a more lightweight ranker that omits the expensive proximity calculations.

Overview of the Available Rankers

Phrase proximity and BM25 are the two most important factors that contribute to the final document weight. However, the final weight value is determined by the ranker, that is, the specific function that crunches one or more factors into a single number (also, there are other factors besides phrase weight and BM25 that Sphinx can compute and use).

As of 1.10-beta, Sphinx has eight different rankers, and will definitely add more in the future. Every ranker computes weight differently and thus might or might not be suitable for a particular scenario.

There are three simple rankers (NONE, WORDCOUNT, and FIELDMASK) that do nothing, count keyword occurrences, and return the matching fields bitmask, respectively. Those are useful when ranking is not needed at all, or are computed in some manner on the application side.

There are two legacy rankers (PROXIMITY and MATCHANY) that rely on phrase proximity alone and are used to emulate ALL and ANY legacy matching modes, respectively.

There are three more rankers (BM25, PROXIMITY_BM25, and SPH04) that can combine phrase proximity, BM25, and other bits. Query-syntax-enabled modes and SphinxQL default to PROXIMITY_BM25 for now, and in case you're still using PROXIMITY for historical reasons, it's strongly suggested that you consider PROXIMITY_BM25 instead (because of better BM25-assisted ordering of the matches that result in the same proximity value, especially useful for one-keyword queries). BM25 is recommended as a reasonably good quick ranker, and also for comparison with other systems. SPH04 builds upon PROXIMITY_BM25 but additionally ranks exact field matches and matches at the beginning of a field higher than other matches.

PROXIMITY_BM25 and SPH04 are expected to yield the best quality, but your particular results may vary.

Your choice of ranker can severely affect search query performance. NONE is obviously the quickest ranker, but what about the others? Processing the keyword positions (occurrences) is typically the most expensive part of the calculation, so rankers that don't need to do that (FIELDMASK and BM25) are always quicker than the others. They utilize less disk I/O because they don't need to access keyword positions. Rankers that process keyword positions (WORDCOUNT, PROXIMITY, MATCHANY, PROXIMITY_BM25, and SPH04) differ among themselves only in CPU impact.

Nitty-gritty Ranker Details

This section describes the exact algorithms Sphinx rankers use and provides pseudo-code. You can skip it freely unless you want to tweak ranking, tune field weights, and perform similar tasks.

While the factors might be integer, Boolean, floating point, or whatever, the weight has to be a single scalar value. In Sphinx, the weight is not just scalar but an integer value. This isn't a real constraint, because floating-point weight values can be mapped to integers in a variety of ways.

Let's begin with the three simplest rankers:

SPH_RANK_NONE
> Just assigns every document weight to 1:
>
> ```
> weight = 1
> ```
>
> Why use this and effectively skip ranking at all? The answer is performance. If you're sorting search results by price, why spend CPU cycles on an expensive ranking you're going to throw away anyway?

SPH_RANK_WORDCOUNT
> Counts all the keyword occurrences and multiplies them by user field weights:
>
> ```
> weight = 0
> foreach ( field in matching_fields )
>     weight += num_keyword_occurrences ( field )
> ```
>
> Note that this ranker counts all occurrences, and not only the unique keywords. Therefore, three occurrences of just one matching keyword will contribute exactly as much as one occurrence of three different keywords.

SPH_RANK_FIELDMASK
> Returns a bit mask of matched fields. It can be particularly useful in conjunction with the BITDOT() function in expressions:
>
> ```
> weight = 0
> foreach ( field in matching_fields )
>     set_bit ( weight, index_of ( field ) )
>     // or in other words, weight |= ( 1 << index_of ( field ) )
> ```

The other five rankers are somewhat more complicated and mostly rely on phrase proximity:

SPH_RANK_PROXIMITY
> This is the default ranker in the SPH_MATCH_ALL legacy mode; it returns the phrase proximity factor as a resultant weight:
>
> ```
> weight = doc_phrase_weight
> ```

By the definition of phrase weight, when documents match the query but no sequence of two keywords matches, all such documents will receive a weight of 1.

That, clearly, isn't differentiating the results much, so using the PROXIMITY_BM25 ranker instead is advised. The associated searching performance impact should be negligible.

SPH_RANK_MATCHANY

This ranker is used to emulate the legacy SPH_MATCH_ANY matching mode. It combines phrase proximity and the number of matched keywords in such a way that, with default per-field weights, a longer subphrase match (a.k.a. bigger phrase proximity) in any field ranks higher, and in case of equal phrase proximity, the document with more matched unique keywords ranks higher. In other words, we look at the maximum subphrase match length first, and a number of unique matched keywords second. Here it is in pseudocode:

```
k = 0
foreach ( field in all_fields )
    k += user_weight ( field ) * num_keywords ( query )

weight = 0
foreach ( field in matching_fields )
{
    field_phrase_weight = max_common_subsequence_length ( query, field )
    field_rank = ( field_phrase_weight * k + num_matching_keywords ( field ) )
    weight += user_weight ( field ) * field_rank
}
```

This ranker does not use BM25 at all because the legacy mode did not use it and we need to stay compatible.

SPH_RANK_PROXIMITY_BM25

This is the default SphinxQL ranker and also the default ranker when "extended" matching mode is used with SphinxAPI. It computes weight as:

```
weight = doc_phrase_weight*1000 + integer(doc_bm25*999)
```

So, document phrase proximity is the primary factor and BM25 is an auxiliary one that additionally sorts documents sharing the same phrase proximity. The result of BM25 is confined to the 0..1 range, so the last three decimal digits of the final weight contain scaled BM25, and all the other digits are used for the phrase weight.

SPH_RANK_BM25

This is the simplified ranker that sums user weights of the matched fields and BM25:

```
field_weights = 0
foreach ( field in matching_fields )
    field_weights += user_weight ( field )
weight = field_weights*1000 + integer(doc_bm25*999)
```

This is almost like the PROXIMITY_BM25 ranker, except that user weights are not multiplied by per-field phrase proximities. Not using phrase proximity allows the engine to evaluate the query using document lists only, and skip the processing of keyword occurrence lists. Unless your documents are extremely short (think tweets, titles, etc.), occurrence lists are somewhat bigger than document lists and take somewhat more time to process. So, BM25 is a faster ranker than any of the proximity-aware ones.

Also, many other search systems either default to the BM25 ranking, or provide it as the only option. So, use the BM25 ranker when doing performance testing to make the comparison fair.

SPH_RANK_SPH04

This ranker further improves on the PROXIMITY_BM25 ranker (and introduces numbers instead of meaningful names, because names that list all ranker features become complicated). Phrase proximity is still the leading factor, but, within a given phrase proximity, matches in the beginning of the field are ranked higher, and exact matches of the entire field are ranked highest. Here is the pseudocode:

```
field_weights = 0
foreach ( field in matching_fields )
{
    f = 4*max_common_subsequence_length ( query, field )
    if ( exact_field_match ( query, field ) )
        f += 3
    else if ( first_keyword_matches ( query, field ) )
        f += 2
    field_weights += f * user_weight ( field )
}
weight = field_weights*1000 + integer(doc_bm25*999)
```

Thus, when querying for **Market Street**, SPH04 will basically rank a document with an exact "Market Street" match in one of the fields the highest, followed by "Market Street Grocery" that begins the field with a matching keyword, then followed by "West Market Street" that has a phrase match somewhere, and then followed by all the documents that mention both keywords but not as a phrase (such as "Flea Market on 26th Street").

How Do I Draw Those Stars?

Or, more formally, how do I compute the maximum possible weight and scale the returned weights to a five-star system, or an A–F scale, or percents, or whatever else?

As you saw in the preceding section, there's no simple way to do that. The maximum weight depends both on a chosen ranker and on a particular query. For example, an upper weight bound with the PROXIMITY_BM25 ranker would be:

```
max_weight = num_keywords * sum ( user_field_weights ) * 1000 + 999
```

But can this upper bound ever be reached? Barely, in practice, because that would require exact phrase matches, in all the fields, plus BM25 peaking at 999, which roughly translates to using only one-in-a-million keywords. Moreover, what if the query uses field limit operators, such as **@title hello world**? In that case, our upper bound can never be reached because we would never match any field except the title field. In this particular query, the practical upper bound that could possibly be reached by an "ideal" document is much lower than the mathematical maximum.

Therefore, computing the "true" maximum weight (one that can actually be reached) is really, really complicated. We could possibly do that on the Sphinx side, but it would be a lengthy R&D project with a questionable outcome. So, if you can't live without percentiles (or stars), you can either use the "absolute" upper bound estimate like the one in the previous equation (which would never be practically reached, so you can't get close to a "100 percent match"), or just use the maximum weight from your particular query, and rescale everything to that weight. Using multiqueries, the latter option can be performed with little overhead.

How Do I Rank Exact Field Matches Higher?

This is a perfect job for the SPH04 ranker, added in version 1.10-beta. You can't do it with either the SphinxAPI-default PROXIMITY ranker or the SphinxQL-default PROXIMITY_BM25 ranker. They just rank a longer subphrase match higher, but do not care where in the field that match occurred, and whether it matched the entire field or not.

How Do I Force Document D to Rank First?

Depending on why document D needs to be ranked higher, you either use a ranker that fits your requirements better, or use Sphinx runtime expressions to compute what you need and sort the result set differently.

For instance, the example of boosting exact field-equals-query matches from the earlier section could be approached by sorting by an expression:

```
SELECT *, @weight+IF(fieldcrc==$querycrc,1000,0) AS myweight ...
ORDER BY myweight DESC
```

where fieldcrc is the CRC(field) attribute computed at indexing time and stored in the index, and querycrc is the CRC(query) computed at searching time. Note that this, unlike the SPH04 ranker, would only boost absolute exact matches, including both case and punctuation (unless you remove case and punctuation manually before computing fieldcrc and querycrc).

Or, to take an entirely different approach, instead of checking for a strict CRC match, you could index and store field lengths, and rank shorter fields higher by using an expression such as this:

```
SELECT *, @weight+ln(len+1)*1000 AS myweight ...
```

In this example, to force a document rank higher when a given keyword is searched for, you create a separate field with super-important keywords, put it there, and assign a high weight to that field. (Don't set the weight higher than 1 million, though, or the 32-bit weight will overflow!)

How Does Sphinx Ranking Compare to System XYZ?

Major web search engines (think Google) are an entirely different story. Web-scale ranking (and spam fighting) forces them to account for hundreds or thousands of factors in their ranking. Many of those factors (PageRank, page and domain age, incoming link count, ratio of code to text, etc.) are not text-related, however, and can also be employed with Sphinx in a particular application by using expressions. Sphinx itself is generic and its rankers just handle some text-related factors; everything else has to be explicitly added on top.

However, most other full-text search systems still either default to plain old BM25 for text-related factors, or even limit you to it. Don't get me wrong, BM25 is a great weighting factor. But using it as the only ranking factor is, ahem, really last century. Sphinx proximity-based rankers do take a step toward improving that, and future versions are bringing even more factors and relevance ranking flexibility.

Where to Go from Here

Congratulations, you've just made a pretty solid jumpstart into searching with Sphinx! We've been through all of the everyday chores and then some (to continue the chores metaphor, some weekend and even a few holiday ones were addressed as well). Getting up and running, writing a proper configuration file to index your data, maintaining the indexes, and querying in a variety of kinds with both SphinxAPI and SphinxQL should all now be a piece of cake to you.

Cakes aren't the only sweets out there, though, and so there's quite a bit more to Sphinx.

Programmers' paths from here would probably diverge. Some sites require extra fine-tuning of indexing and searching with more advanced features; some need to scale both up and out; some are eager to find more about Sphinx's extra perks, such as snippets.

But even "just" the intricacies of indexing do not end here, by far. There are advanced text processing options: tokenizing exceptions, morphology helpers (stemmers and word form dictionaries), ignored and blended characters, 1-gram indexing for CJK searching support, prefix and infix indexing for substring searching support, and more. There are more indexing tricks to distribute the documents evenly, throttle the impact on the disk and database, fine-tune certain index size/performance trade-offs, and so forth.

Speaking of which, there's somewhat more to searching speed fine-tuning as well, from performance-impacting knobs (such as index caching and buffer size controls) via useful optimization tricks (virtual keywords, filter reordering, reverse scans) all the way up to full-blown advanced features (multiquery batches and the resultant possibilities for inter-query and intra-query optimization).

Then there's the separate big topic of parallel and distributed searching and search cluster setup and maintenance, which inevitably bobs up sooner or later as you grow.

And then a few more topics big and small: real-time indexes, SphinxSE (the embedded storage engine client that plugs into MySQL or MariaDB), creating snippets, building clusters of related documents, implementing keyword suggestions, and on and on.

Regrettably, this particular publication is too narrow to contain all that marvelous jazz, but hopefully, with your help, we're opening a series on Sphinx here rather than doing a one-off publication. So, get back in touch, and let us know what of the aforementioned topics would be of most interest for a sequel (or any other feedback you might have, which is always appreciated).

And hey, thanks for choosing Sphinx!

Get even more for your money.

Join the O'Reilly Community, and register the O'Reilly books you own. It's free, and you'll get:

- $4.99 ebook upgrade offer
- 40% upgrade offer on O'Reilly print books
- Membership discounts on books and events
- Free lifetime updates to ebooks and videos
- Multiple ebook formats, DRM FREE
- Participation in the O'Reilly community
- Newsletters
- Account management
- 100% Satisfaction Guarantee

Signing up is easy:

1. **Go to: oreilly.com/go/register**
2. **Create an O'Reilly login.**
3. **Provide your address.**
4. **Register your books.**

Note: English-language books only

To order books online:
oreilly.com/store

For questions about products or an order:
orders@oreilly.com

To sign up to get topic-specific email announcements and/or news about upcoming books, conferences, special offers, and new technologies:
elists@oreilly.com

For technical questions about book content:
booktech@oreilly.com

To submit new book proposals to our editors:
proposals@oreilly.com

O'Reilly books are available in multiple DRM-free ebook formats. For more information:
oreilly.com/ebooks

O'REILLY®

Spreading the knowledge of innovators | oreilly.com

The information you need, when and where you need it.

With Safari Books Online, you can:

Access the contents of thousands of technology and business books

- Quickly search over 7000 books and certification guides
- Download whole books or chapters in PDF format, at no extra cost, to print or read on the go
- Copy and paste code
- Save up to 35% on O'Reilly print books
- **New!** Access mobile-friendly books directly from cell phones and mobile devices

Stay up-to-date on emerging topics before the books are published

- Get on-demand access to evolving manuscripts.
- Interact directly with authors of upcoming books

Explore thousands of hours of video on technology and design topics

- Learn from expert video tutorials
- Watch and replay recorded conference sessions

CPSIA information can be obtained at www.ICGtesting.com
Printed in the USA
BVOW081036260312

286062BV00004B/25/P